A World o[f] Business Transformation at Xerox

Xerox Quality Services

Reproduction or translation of any part of this work
beyond that permitted by Section 107 or 108 of the
1976 United States Copyright Act without the permission
of the copyright owner is unlawful. Requests for
permission or further information should be addressed to
XQS Press, Xerox Quality Services, Xerox Corporation.
80 Linden Oaks Parkway (804-02A)
Rochester, NY 14625

This publication is designed to provide accurate and
authorative information in regard to the subject
matter covered. It is sold with the understanding that
the publisher is not engaged in rendering legal, accounting,
or other professional services. If legal advice or other
expert assistance is required, the services of a competent
professional person should be sought. *From a Declaration
of Principles jointly adopted by a Committee of the
American Bar Association and a Committee of Publishers.*

Library of Congress Cataloging-in-Publication Data:

A World of Quality: the timeless passport / edited by Richard C.
    Palermo and Gregory H. Watson
        p. cm.
      ISBN 0-87389-290-9   ISBN 0-7863-0803-6
      1. Xerox Corporation–Quality control.   2. Copying machine
    industry–United States–Quality control.   I. Palermo, Richard C.
    II. Watson, Gregory H.
    HD9802.3.U62W67   1993
    338.7'68611-dc20   93-35607
                                                                  CIP

Printed in the United States of America.
123456BS109876

Dedication

To Team Xerox: The Xerox customers, employees, and suppliers, world-wide, who have joined hands in this memorable and continuing quality journey.

Preface

The creation of this book, in many ways, was an exercise in the use of Total Quality Management (TQM) principles and practices. A small group of Xerox people, from different work areas, with diverse backgrounds, having different tenure with the company, even from different generations, came together in a team effort, with a single purpose: To produce a book that will enlighten and encourage others to start, or continue on, the quality journey, a journey toward fully satisfied and even delighted customers, clients, patients, students, or constituencies; served by motivated and energized people; for the benefit of their stockholders, owners, sponsors, or supporters. The use of these multiple terms was carefully considered. They are meant to indicate to the reader that TQM can work for all enterprises or undertakings in all parts of the world, anytime. *A World of Quality: The Timeless Passport* is the story of the global pursuit of quality by Xerox to stimulate increased business performance in a changing business environment.

This book, with its details about Japanese, American, and European quality efforts, clearly shows that TQM principles and practices transcend language and cultural differences.

The Xerox team came together and accepted the book-writing challenge. The team broke into work groups, divided responsibilities, designed a management process, problem solved issues, and produced a draft manuscript in less than two months. The secret? The team members had been trained in TQM and had been nurtured in a quality atmosphere to become dedicated practitioners of TQM.

Imagine the power of hundreds, thousands, or even hundreds of thousands of people who are similarly skilled in TQM. This truly represents the promise of TQM—a capability to efficiently and effectively focus a powerfully diverse set of talents on the objective of understanding and satisfying requirements, and continuously improving without end.

The book writing team included the following people:

Paul Allaire
Barbara Ficarra
Derek Hanley
Donna Harman
John Kelsch
Dick Leo
Sam Malone
Bob Osterhoff
Dick Palermo
Karen Sliva
Greg Watson
Masataka Yoshizawa

Others contributed through technical and editorial review:

Nick Argona
Joe Cahalan
John Cooney
Tony Costanza
David Nadler
Frank Pipp
Norm Rickard
Mark Shimelonis

Still others contributed through administration and project support:

Dan Holahan
Gary Mroczek
Jim Reinhard
Carole Tomczyk
Paul Wetenhall

The objective of the team was to capture the interest of the widest audience possible and to provide valuable and historical insights, by detailing the following:

- An historical overview of the Xerox quality journey (chapter one).

- The quality pursuit beginning in Japan with Fuji Xerox and the Deming Prize (chapter two).

- The strategic quality plan for the United States—the "Green Book" (chapter three).

- The American challenge of the Baldrige Award (chapter four).

- Ongoing assessments used to reinitiate the momentum in the quality journey (chapter five).

- The European effort toward the European Quality Award (chapter six).

- Thoughtful lessons learned along the journey (chapter seven).

- A look to the future by Paul A. Allaire, C.E.O. of Xerox Corporation (chapter eight).

We hope that the following eight chapters fulfill our objective. We would love to hear from our customers in order to continuously improve. Please call or write Xerox using the contact information provided at the end of the book.

August 1, 1993   Richard C. Palermo, Sr.
Rochester, NY   Gregory H. Watson
                                            Editors

Contents

Chapter One
Discovering New Perspectives

Many in the business world know something of the Xerox quality story: Xerox had serious business problems in the mid-1970s through the early 1980s but then improved the quality of its products to recapture a portion of the market share that had been lost to the Japanese. What is not quite as well known, however, are the details behind this turnaround, specifically:

- Why Xerox came so close to catastrophe
- How Xerox changed its business using Total Quality Management
- How Xerox developed its focus for the future

The problems Xerox faced did not happen overnight; they built up over a long time. Likewise, the answers did not magically appear. Not all elements of the Xerox quality program, as it exists today, were created at one point in time. Although some elements were part of the original strategy, many were developed in response to a specific event or circumstance. As Xerox progressed on its quality journey and gained additional insights, it modified its strategy to reflect what it had learned. The advantage of this strategy: 100,000 people were trained in a common language and in the quality process, and were encouraged to use these tools to improve and produce an astounding array of business changes and innovations.

The model of business success: the late 1960s and early 1970s

During the early days, Xerox experienced very rapid growth. This growth resulted from the introduction of the 914—the first plain paper copier—which was based on a new technology, xerography. It was a product customers were waiting in line to use. With the introduction of the 914, Xerox created a new industry.

By the time the competition entered the marketplace in the early 1970s, Xerox was generating record levels of profit and revenue. In the mid-1970s, the return on assets (ROA) generated by Xerox averaged in the low twenty percent range. This high level of profitability focused much attention on the Xerox business. Competition became only one of several major business issues that demanded the company's attention.

- In the early 1970s, IBM and Kodak entered the copier business and went after the same lucrative segments of the market created by Xerox. Xerox wrongly believed these two giants were the main competitive threat.

- The Japanese entered the market with low-volume machines that delivered reliable, high-quality equipment in a market segment Xerox had virtually ignored. Their performance allowed them to build a stronghold and later move upmarket into the heartland of the Xerox business.

- A number of antitrust lawsuits kept the Xerox management team distracted from the business end of company operations.

- In the 1970s, Xerox was caught off guard by the Federal Trade Commission (FTC), which accused Xerox of illegally monopolizing the office copier business. After negotiations with the FTC, Xerox agreed to open approximately 1,700 patents to its competitors. Later, Xerox agreed to limit some pricing practices and patent licensing arrangements as well. Xerox also agreed to provide technical assistance to those organizations that wanted to use these patents.

The cumulative effect of these issues caused the Xerox market share to fall from approximately eighty-five percent in the late 1970s to approximately forty percent over the next several years. However, even during these turbulent times, Xerox continued to report strong revenues and profits. As a result, it was difficult to recognize the impact these changes had upon the company, because the profits masked the actual business performance.

Fuji Xerox and the New Xerox Movement

These adverse business trends had already been detected in Japan at the Xerox subsidiary, Fuji Xerox. Fuji Xerox was a joint venture created by Fuji Photo Film and Rank Xerox in 1962. In the early 1970s, Fuji Xerox had begun to experience the onslaught of competition in their home markets and had conducted several studies of its competitive position. At that time, Fuji Xerox estimated it was approximately twenty-five percent off the mark of its Japanese competitors for manufacturing costs.

To address this issue, Fuji Xerox began implementing its quality journey, the principles of Total Quality Management (TQM), in 1976. Fuji Xerox called this journey the New Xerox Movement. This effort resulted in Fuji Xerox receiving the Deming Prize and making substantial improvements of its business position. (The pursuit of the Deming Prize by Fuji Xerox is described in chapter two.)

In the late 1970s, Yotaro "Tony" Kobayashi, President of Fuji Xerox, encouraged Xerox executives to look at their comparative cost analysis and take action. After examining the Fuji Xerox comparative studies, Xerox believed that comparing its United States operations to those of Fuji Xerox and its Japanese competitors would provide an excellent assessment of its current competitive position. This study was conducted by internal engineers from both the design and manufacturing functions, and it provided Xerox with a baseline for comparison of its low volume copier products against their Japanese competition. The results of this pioneering benchmarking effort, which took place in 1979, were met with dismay and disbelief:

- The ratio of indirect workers to direct workers at the United States operations was twice that of the best Japanese competitor.

- Xerox used almost double the number of workers to develop a new product.

- It took Xerox twice as long to develop new products.

- It took Xerox nearly three times longer to deliver new products to the marketplace.

The benchmarking provided additional insights about Japanese competitors. These included:

- Defect levels of Xerox equipment were approximately seven times higher than those of its Japanese competitors.

- On average, the Japanese selling price of equipment in the United States almost equaled the Xerox Unit Manufacturing Cost (UMC), and the Japanese were making a profit.

From 1980 to 1983, evidence that Xerox was in trouble continued to mount:

- Market share continued to decline.

- The Xerox ROA slipped from nineteen percent in 1980 to below ten percent by the end of 1982.

- Over 20,000 positions were eliminated worldwide through initiatives such as early retirement programs and both voluntary and involuntary reductions in force (RIF).

- Levels of management were removed and promotional opportunities diminished.

- Wages were frozen in 1983.

- The decline in ROA greatly reduced employee profit sharing.

- New product delivery stagnated.

- Employee satisfaction began to slip as people lost confidence in the abilities of senior management.

Xerox was not completely taken by surprise, however, and it had already taken actions to counter this reversal in business fortune. For instance, in 1980, the union representing the Xerox production work force, the Amalgamated Clothing and Textile Workers Union (ACTWU), recognized that in order to protect its constituents, Xerox must remain competitive. The union had witnessed the demise of the clothing industry in America and knew that the problems Xerox was experiencing could result in the same negative outcome.

During the 1980 contract negotiations, the union and Xerox forged an agreement regarding employee involvement, which was called Quality of Work Life. This followed several years of research into Japanese Quality Circles and other employee involvement strategies and techniques. This concept of employee involvement became an important catalyst for turning the business around.

In 1981, Xerox combined the concepts of benchmarking and employee involvement into a productivity initiative called Business Effectiveness. This effort focused on reducing costs and improving the financial picture of the company. The phrase, "do it once and do it right," became the slogan, although no enablers were provided that would allow people to work smarter. In fact, most employees felt they were already working hard, and as a result, they became increasingly frustrated by the demands to do more. All of these efforts—Quality of Work Life, employee involvement, and benchmarking of product costing—were not enough to counter the competitive challenge.

Meanwhile, in 1982, David Kearns, the newly appointed chief executive officer of Xerox, had been witnessing firsthand the implementation of TQM at Fuji Xerox. During one of his return trips from Japan, Kearns began listing the factors that made the Japanese better than their American counterparts. After eliminating those factors that he felt were not significant, three elements remained: cost, quality, and expectations. Moreover, Kearns noticed that the Japanese set much higher expectations for their perform-ance and output than the United States operations did—not by a little, but by a lot!

At about the same time, Kearns was approached by a few Xerox employees who urged the use of a TQM approach to address these business needs. To put these findings into action, Kearns commissioned eleven people to explore and outline a TQM approach for Xerox. This design team would draft a "vision book" that would outline how the company would look if TQM efforts were successful. The intent was to construct a strategy that would be broad enough and deep enough to turn the competitive tide.

The birth of Leadership Through Quality

As the design team developed its quality vision book over the next several months, it became apparent that operational changes alone would not be enough for success. For Xerox to reach the improvement objective, changes in behaviors and attitudes throughout the entire company would also be required. This realization prompted the team to recommend retaining an expert in the field of behavioral change. David Nadler, President of Delta Consulting, was selected to assist the team through organizational change issues and to help communicate these issues to senior management. This was the beginning of an enduring relationship which continues today.

Nadler coached management to understand that they should expect resistance to the recommended changes. This resistance, he said, would not be driven by technological issues but by behavioral issues. Nadler believed that it was critical to support the desired behavioral and cultural changes through a variety of approaches. Thus, the design team focused on what was often referred to as the six "levers of change." These were:

- Senior management behavior

- Communication

- Training

- Reward and recognition

- Standards and measures

- Transition team

Unless all of these factors were addressed together, any attempt at basic change would have been isolated and subsequently rejected by the old system.

The efforts of the design team resulted in a draft notebook that was shared with the top twenty-five Xerox executives attending a meeting at the Xerox Training Center in Leesburg, Virginia. The purpose of this February 1983 meeting was to engage the worldwide Xerox senior management team in developing a change strategy that was specific to the Xerox culture and needs.

By Kearns' direction, there were three absolutes of this quality strategy:

- Xerox was going to initiate a TQM approach.

- Xerox would take the time to design it right the first time.

- It would involve all employees.

A set of discussion-provoking questions was developed by the design team. These questions would help direct the progress of the management team in developing the details of its commitment to quality. This discussion aid included such questions as:

- Is there agreement on the principles, tools, and management actions on which the definition of quality is based?

- Is the proposed problem-solving process accepted as basic to the concept and part of the definition?

- Do we believe that five years is a realistic time period in which to achieve a state of maturity?

- Is there agreement on the need to provide quality training for all Xerox employees?

- How will quality be incorporated into the management process?

- By what name should the Xerox total quality strategy be known?

The resulting output of this team's work included the Xerox Quality Policy.

Xerox is a quality company. Quality is the basic business principle for Xerox. Quality means providing our external and internal customers with innovative products and services that fully satisfy their requirements. Quality improvement is the job of every Xerox employee.

The quality policy established during this 1983 meeting has not been changed and still guides the operating philosophy of Xerox today.

The development of Leadership Through Quality

After the first Leesburg meeting, the senior management team personally took responsibility for communicating the quality direction and serving as the role model for deployment of Leadership Through Quality. Leadership Through Quality became the agreed upon strategy that would be used to turn around the three most significant business challenges which Xerox faced in 1983:

- No true customer focus—Customer satisfaction and customer opinions were not actively pursued in order to include their requirements for running the business.

- Costs—Product production costs were too high.

- Lack of market-connectedness—Product development was based on capability rather than marketplace need.

Leadership Through Quality was also the strategy for changing the Xerox culture which would focus and empower employees to:

- Meet customer requirements

- Drive business priorities

- Continuously improve

The development of Leadership Through Quality was an intensive effort. Three major efforts were identified to make Leadership Through Quality fully operational.

First, it was essential for the quality initiative to fit into the unique Xerox environment. To coordinate the deployment of Leadership Through Quality, management decided that the corporation needed a quality focal point within each organizational unit, as well as a focal point for the entire company. Quality was not going to be a separate department or function. Management also thought that the individuals selected for these quality positions would send a strong signal to employees of how serious management really was. To this end, management appointed high growth potential individuals as quality officers in each operating unit and a corporate vice president of quality. Together, these individuals formed the Quality Implementation Team (QIT) that was charged with researching and designing the implementation specifics of the Xerox approach to quality.

The QIT worked for approximately six months on its assignment. As part of their research effort, QIT members consulted renowned quality experts such as W. Edwards Deming, Joseph M. Juran, and Philip B. Crosby. They benchmarked companies with quality initiatives in effect, including Corning, Ford Motor Company, Hewlett-Packard and IBM. Pieces of each were adapted to fit into a quality mosaic that was specific to Xerox, and complemented its strengths and important areas of need.

During this research and design phase, the team members reviewed their progress with unit management and solicited input for strengthening the quality strategy. This input was then shared with management as a whole. This approach helped to ensure a wider acceptance of the final strategy throughout the management ranks. The output created was the Xerox Green Book, which outlined all of the elements of Leadership Through Quality and set the goals and expectations for the quality journey. (A synopsis of the Green Book is contained in chapter three.)

Second, because Xerox management understood that training was critical to the success of the quality effort, it formed a twelve-member Quality Education and Training Council. The council, whose members came from the various Xerox training organizations around the world, spent several months designing the supporting training program which would provide employees with the quality skills and tools that they needed to use for addressing the business issues.

Since its introduction in the first quarter of 1984, the Leadership Through Quality training program has been translated into fourteen languages to ensure a common approach to quality training at all Xerox facilities worldwide. The only exception was Fuji Xerox, which had its own materials prepared and deployed in the late 1970s as part of the New Xerox Movement. The widespread use of common Leadership Through Quality training has proven to be one of the most important aspects of the Leadership Through Quality implementation strategy.

Third, management needed to extend its commitment to Leadership Through Quality. To achieve this, Xerox leaders met again in Leesburg in August 1983. This time, approximately 120 people, including the original twenty-five team members plus the next two levels of the upper management team, convened to review and obtain support for the final strategy. After reaching consensus on the overall approach, each unit finalized its own implementation plans. Kearns set the example of active involvement of management in the support of the Leadership Through Quality deployment effort. He initiated the training cascade by leading his family group (his seven direct reports) through six and a half days of Leadership Through Quality training. After the completion of this training, they were required to participate in an on-the-job improvement project within their family group to apply the newly learned tools, thus reinforcing these new skills and techniques of quality.

The deployment journey

Although Leadership Through Quality took eighteen months to develop, the training of 100,000 Xerox employees took over four years to complete. To deploy Leadership Through Quality, an innovative strategy to cascade the training by family group through the organization, level by level, was used. This model was called the Learn-Use-Teach-Inspect (LUTI) model of training. This proved to be effective in deploying the training and practicing of Leadership Through Quality without losing the substance of the methods. Figure 1.1 illustrates this training strategy.

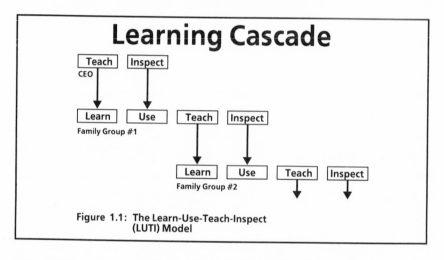

Figure 1.1: The Learn-Use-Teach-Inspect
(LUTI) Model

Following the LUTI model, a team is first trained by its manager in the principles, methods, and tools of Leadership Through Quality. Xerox training professionals assist the manager in delivering the training. The second step is to use the training to address business challenges immediately after the training is provided. Team members use what they have learned in training to attack a problem within their own area. In the third step, each manager, now experienced in the use of the tools, trains his or her direct reports using the standard Leadership Through Quality materials. In the final step, the manager inspects each of the direct report's application projects. (In Xerox, the term "inspection" means to monitor, assess, and coach rather than the traditional meaning of measuring against a fixed standard of goodness.)

During this four-year deployment period, Xerox had to weather continued downward trends and business pressures. However, the effort paid off. In addition to being a strategy for change within Xerox, Leadership Through

Quality also proved to be a tool for measuring progress in business improvement. By 1987, the people of Xerox had reversed the decline in market share and ROA. The majority of Xerox employees had been trained—and were using—Leadership Through Quality in their daily work processes.

The 1987 quality assessment and the Baldrige Award

Xerox came to understand the importance of periodic assessments in order to provide an opportunity for reflection and to stimulate future initiatives. The key to business success, after all, was in the reinforcement of both the commitment and the pursuit of continuous improvement.

The first assessment at Xerox was conducted in 1987 shortly after Paul A. Allaire became president of the company. The purpose of this assessment was to evaluate the progress in deployment of Leadership Through Quality and to compare the quality results against the goals established in 1983. The objective was to measure and define gaps in quality implementation against the plan and to gain insight into why progress was not being achieved at a faster pace.

To complete the data collection phase of the assessment, the Corporate Quality Office engaged Delta Consulting to help design a survey that would be distributed to a cross section of managers; numerous interviews were conducted throughout Xerox, and employee feedback results were gathered. The analysis of this data yielded both strengths and areas for improvement.

Strengths of the 1987 assessment were:

- The strategy was fundamentally sound.

- There was worldwide support for the strategy.

- Meetings, teamwork, and group effectiveness showed the most improvement.

- Success and areas of excellence contributed to employee satisfaction.

There were many examples of individual managers, across a wide range of functions and on a worldwide basis, who were making a difference in the business by using the principles and tools of quality. These people helped disprove the argument that while quality could be made to work in Japan, it might not work elsewhere. They became the role models that others sought to emulate.

Xerox also had made good progress on what it needed most: teamwork. Xerox people were beginning to listen a lot better—especially to customers. This behavior change, combined with the disciplined use of quality tools, was helping to solve problems faster and more effectively by getting to the root cause of the issues. The advertising theme "Team Xerox" was originally used to describe groupings of new products. It was later adapted to Leadership Through Quality as an accurate characterization of the way Xerox employees were beginning to behave by mid-1987. Since then, "Team Xerox" has become more widely recognized as a call for Xerox people to exercise the quality methods through participative team efforts to improve processes and increase customer satisfaction.

Areas for improvement uncovered during the 1987 assessment included the following:

- Quality was not integrated into the basic business process. It was still a management topic rather than the way things were done.

- Pressure for near-term financial results was overriding the quality focus.

- Specific weaknesses were identified in the following categories:
  — Role models—not many were apparent
  — Inspection and coaching—not enough
  — Recognition, reward, and penalties—often weighted against old values
  — Use of the Leadership Through Quality tools and processes—not deployed sufficiently
  — Benchmarking—not universally used

In addition, there were not enough examples of line managers who were improving business results by using the quality process. When business pressures for profit performance increased, quality principles sometimes became secondary considerations. This was especially true in the trade-off between financial performance and customer satisfaction. All three corporate priorites—return on assets (ROA), market share, and customer satisfaction—supposedly had equal importance. In reality, management was emphasizing ROA as the primary goal and priority. This finding in itself justified the assessment effort and resulted in a customer satisfaction white paper, which was prepared by a cross-functional team using the standard six-step problem-solving process deployed in the Leadership Through Quality training.

In response to this assessment, senior management prioritized the three fundamental corporate goals to reflect the objectives of Leadership Through Quality:

1. Customer satisfaction
2. ROA
3. Market Share

Senior management believed that a stronger customer focus would build market share and profits over time. Putting customer satisfaction first was a major symbolic change for Xerox, and it set the stage for a change in ongoing business operations reviews. The reviews would become the forum for "in-process" assessments of quality progress at Xerox, and they would be conducted from a customer-focused perspective.

The timing of this renewed focus on the customer coincided with the celebration of the fiftieth anniversary of the invention of xerography on October 22, 1988. This was particularly fitting because the founders had established a tradition that focused on delivering value to the customer. This was also the first year companies could apply for the Malcolm Baldrige National Quality Award—an award that recognizes excellence in delivering customer satisfaction. Xerox management seriously considered its readiness to apply for the Baldrige Award during the first year of competition. However, management recognized that the true value of the application submission was in its effect as a stimulant for "tuning up" the Xerox quality system during the preparation process. There was not enough time to prepare an application during the first Baldrige Award cycle, so management postponed the application decision for review during the second Baldrige Award cycle.

Why apply for a quality award? Xerox managers came to understand that some periodic interventions were required to stimulate and to refocus an organization. Management had evidence that the experience of applying for quality awards, and having to respond to each part of the award criteria, would help Xerox continue to address the quality issues identified in the 1987 assessment. The assessment process, as laid out by the various criteria for the different quality awards, proved to be an excellent business improvement tool. For instance, in applying for the Deming Prize, Fuji Xerox had gained critical insights. Other Xerox units have similarly benefited through their pursuit of various quality awards. By the end of 1988, Xerox had been successful in its pursuit of five national quality awards (the Netherlands, France, two in Britain, and Japan). Management believed that Xerox would achieve similar benefits from an external evaluation as conducted by the Baldrige examiners. The application process would provide the vehicle necessary for improvement.

In December 1988, Xerox senior management decided that the company would complete a Baldrige application, but submit it only if Xerox had adequately responded to the award criteria. If the application did not meet the Xerox quality standard, management reasoned, the process of answering the award criteria would still be a useful self-assessment activity. Senior management selected a team that would gather information and write the application. As it generated the application document and coordinated the site visits, the Xerox National Quality Award (NQA) Team kept a record of the problem areas it discovered. The team eventually identified 513 opportunities in the Xerox quality system. These "warts," as they were called, were not eliminated during the process of drafting the application but served as the basis for directing Xerox to the next level of its quality journey once the application was complete. (The Xerox Baldrige Award effort is described in chapter four.)

Business results continued to improve as a result of the deployment of Leadership Through Quality, and the renewed focus on quality and customer satisfaction in the 1987 to 1989 period paid off. Business improvement resulted in return on assets over ten percent for the first time since 1981, and customer satisfaction reached slightly higher than eighty-six percent—up from approximately forty-eight percent in 1985, but still fourteen percent from the desired state. (Note: In the Xerox system for scoring customer satisfaction, a neutral response is counted with negative responses so this fourteen percent is the sum of neutral and negative responses.)

Beyond the Baldrige

The problem areas in the company's performance that were identified during the Baldrige application process formed the basis for the next stage of the quality improvement effort—Intensification. Quality Intensification occurred between 1989 and 1993. It focused on the development and company-wide expansion of two major initiatives: internal quality assessment and more rigorous use of policy deployment. (The evolution of these two initiatives is described in chapter five.) These were deployed in the operating units. In 1992, Rank Xerox demonstrated how these initiatives were integrated with the basic elements of Leadership Through Quality through its successful application for the European Quality Award. Rank Xerox became the first winner of this award. (The pursuit of this award is described in chapter six.)

In 1993, as Xerox reflects back upon the ten-year journey for Leadership Through Quality, the success is evident. Customer satisfaction was up to ninety-two percent and ROA reached almost fifteen percent for 1992 year-

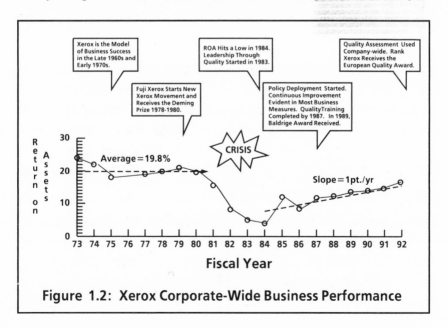

Figure 1.2: Xerox Corporate-Wide Business Performance

end results. Figure 1.2 shows how the journey positively influenced the company's profitability during this decade.

Today, Xerox holds a respected position in American industry and is recognized as "world-class" in many of its operations. Xerox is the only company in the world to have been recognized as a quality leader by the award of the Deming Prize, the Malcolm Baldrige National Quality Award, and the European Quality Award. Xerox is also one of the few companies to regain market share lost to the Japanese without the assistance of government support in the form of subsidies, quotas or tariffs. However, Xerox is not satisfied with its achievements; it still seeks selected "breakthrough" improvements combined with general constantly evolving improvements to maintain its leadership position.

Looking to the future

The final two chapters of this book provide reflective analyses on the lessons learned by Xerox in the pursuit of quality. Chapter seven is a perspective on the changes that have been effected as a result of the quality journey. It represents the cumulative lessons learned from the perspective of Xerox quality officers and, as such, it offers valuable insights. The final chapter is the perspective of Xerox Chairman and Chief Executive Officer Paul A. Allaire as he looks back upon the achievements of Xerox and looks forward to the challenges ahead.

During the pursuit of the Baldrige Award, Allaire had challenged all Xerox units to apply for each of the quality awards for which they were eligible. He further challenged the operating managers to support the development of quality awards in countries that did not currently have them. This is the type of practice that stimulates quality awareness and improvement within Xerox, while externally supporting the improvement of quality and productivity as an international imperative.

To date, Xerox has been successful in applications for fourteen national quality awards throughout the world. It is not the attainment of these awards that makes the difference, rather, it is the preparation and the stimulus from exposure to external review that causes each business unit to excel. In the end, the winner is the customer, both in terms of higher quality products and services and a heightened responsiveness by Xerox to their needs.

Making breakthrough improvements in business performance over the past ten years—doubling the level of customer satisfaction, return on assets, and market share while satisfying Xerox employees—is one result of Leadership Through Quality. This balanced improvement of all four Xerox priorities indicates that quality does not need to be considered a trade-off with business profitability or performance. The Xerox experience shows that quality is the enabler for business success. For Xerox, increased productivity and an improved competitive position will be achieved using ever-improved methods and practices of Leadership Through Quality in a renewed commitment to continuous business improvement.

Chapter Two
Acquiring the Tools

In June 1950, the Union of Japanese Scientists and Engineers (JUSE) invited W. Edwards Deming to present a series of lectures on the applications of statistics in quality control. During a two-month period, Deming taught the applications of statistics as well as the theory and application of statistical sampling. These seminars became the stimulus for the early development of Total Quality Management in Japan.

The following year, JUSE created the Deming Prize to formally honor the friendship, achievements, and contributions of Deming to the improvement of industrial quality control in Japan.

It has become customary in Japan for companies wishing to improve their business performance to challenge the Deming Prize as a means to deliver better products and services. This is done not only for the prestige of the award, but also to benefit from internal improvements that result from the implementation of the company-wide quality control (Total Quality Management) methods needed to qualify for the award. Since 1987, JUSE has opened the competition for the Deming Prize to include companies outside of Japan.

The JUSE Deming Prize Committee awards three Deming prizes. The first is the Deming Prize for Individuals. It is awarded to a person who has made a significant achievement in the theory and application of quality control, or to a person who has made an outstanding contribution to the dissemination of information about statistical quality control. Application for the Deming Prize for Individuals may be made by the individual or by recommendation. Approximately fifty-five individuals have received this award.

The second Deming Prize is offered in three categories: for large businesses as a whole, for divisions of large businesses, and for small businesses. Eligible applicants include public institutions and both public and private companies that have achieved distinction in performance improvement by implementing statistically-based, company-wide quality control. The division award is for corporate divisions of large businesses. The small enterprise award is for small to medium-sized businesses. To apply for the Deming Prize as a division, the following conditions must be met:

- The division must exercise independent management and have full business responsibility for people, facilities, and capital.

- The division must have the responsibility and authority to assure consistent quality control.

- The division must have responsibility for profit and business results improvement for the future.

Applicants for the Deming Prize are required to submit a completed application form and an explanation report—a detailed description of the present situation of the company—to the Deming Prize Committee. The committee then makes a preliminary judgment, which is based on the explanation report. If the application is accepted, a site inspection is scheduled. It is customary for counselors from JUSE, the Japanese Standards Association (JSA), or another quality organization to assist and coach a company through the preparation period. The period is dedicated to developing the applicant's statistical capability. It can take from three to five years from the time a company first decides to challenge the Deming Prize to the time the prize is granted. In fact, it is more appropriate to say that a company prepares for a Deming Prize, rather than applies for it.

The third category is the Quality Control Award for Factory. This prize is awarded to the factory that has had significant success in implementing statistical quality control. The application and examination process is the same as that of the Deming Prize.

Since 1951, only 140 Deming Prizes have been awarded in the second and third categories, averaging just over three a year. Only one company outside of Japan has been recognized with a Deming Prize: Florida Power & Light (United States) in 1989. The Deming Prize for individuals has been awarded only to Japanese nationals.

Prize criteria

The main objective of the examination is to verify that good results are being comprehensively achieved through the implementation of company-wide quality control. Emphasis is placed on the company's potential to continually pursue company-wide quality control. The Deming Prize criteria also emphasize the use of suitable quality control methods based upon considerations such as industry type, company size, and other conditions of the applicant.

In 1954, Armand V. Feigenbaum defined Total Quality Control (TQC) as "the design, production and supply of products or services of the quality level demanded by the customer, at an economically acceptable cost." (TQC is called Total Quality Management (TQM) in most Western countries.) This definition was modified for the application in Japan to include the involvement of all people and all functions in the company, working together to satisfy the customer.

The fundamental emphasis of TQC is on customer satisfaction, together with attention to the public welfare. Also implied in company-wide quality control is an increased understanding and application of statistical concepts and methods by all members of the company. Statistical methods should be used throughout the product or service development and delivery sequence, which includes research, development, design, purchasing, manufacture, inspection, sales, and service. The Deming Prize Committee examines all of these areas for quality control.

Other activities are also subject to examination for quality assurance:

- New product development
- Administration of research and development
- Control of materials and supplies
- Management of physical facilities
- Instrumentation control
- Management of subcontracted work
- Personnel education and training

In addition, the Deming Prize Committee evaluates related activities inside and outside the company, testing the rational reiteration of planning, implementation, evaluation, and improvement of business goals (this reflects the Deming cycle of Plan-Do-Check-Act).

The examiners inspect for the application of company-wide quality control based on statistical methods. They use the following checklist to assess every segment of the company. (In these criteria, the word "policy" is used to mean key business objectives for the entire company.)

1. Company Policy and Planning for Key Business Objectives
    1.1 Policy pursued for management, quality, and quality control
    1.2 Method of establishing policies
    1.3 Appropriateness and consistency of the policies
    1.4 Use of statistical methods
    1.5 Communication, alignment, coordination, and deployment of policies
    1.6 Review of policy implementation and the results achieved
    1.7 Relationship between policies and long- and short-range plans

2. Organization and its Management
    2.1 Explicitness of the scopes of authority and responsibility
    2.2 Appropriateness of delegation of authority
    2.3 Interdivisional cooperation
    2.4 Activities of committees
    2.5 Utilization of the staff
    2.6 Utilization of Quality Control Circle (QC Circle) activities
    2.7 Quality control diagnostic audit

3. QC Education and its Dissemination
    3.1 Education plans, programs, and results
    3.2 Awareness of quality control and degree of understanding of quality control
    3.3 Teaching of statistical concepts and methods, and the extent of their dissemination
    3.4 Understanding of the effectiveness of quality control
    3.5 Education of related companies (subcontractors, suppliers, and distributors)
    3.6 QC Circle activities
    3.7 Suggestion system and its implementation

4. Collection, Dissemination, and Use of Quality Information
    4.1 Collection of external information
    4.2 Transmission of information between divisions
    4.3 Speed of information transmission (use of computers)

4.4 Statistical and analytical techniques applied to information, and the use of these results

5. Analysis
   5.1 Selection of key problems and themes
   5.2 Appropriateness of the analytical approach
   5.3 Use of statistical methods
   5.4 Linkage of analysis with proprietary technology
   5.5 Quality analysis, process analysis
   5.6 Use of analytical results
   5.7 Positiveness of suggestions for improvement

6. Standardization
   6.1 System of standardization
   6.2 Procedure for establishing, revising, and abolishing standards
   6.3 Actual records of the maintenance of standards
   6.4 Contents of the standards
   6.5 Use of statistical methods
   6.6 Accumulation of technology
   6.7 Application of standards

7. Control ("Kanri")
   7.1 Systems for the control of quality and related matters such as cost, delivery, and quantity
   7.2 Control items and control points
   7.3 Use of statistical methods, such as control charts, and the general acceptance of the statistical way of thinking
   7.4 Contribution to performance of QC Circle activities
   7.5 Actual conditions of control activities
   7.6 Actual condition of control state

8. Quality Assurance
   8.1 Procedure for the development of new products and services (quality function deployment and its analysis, reliability management and design review, et cetera)
   8.2 Safety and product liability prevention
   8.3 Process design, process analysis, process control and continuous improvement ("Kaizen")
   8.4 Process capabilities

8.5 Measurement and inspection capabilities and control

8.6 Equipment maintenance and control of subcontracting, purchasing, and services

8.7 Quality assurance system and its audit

8.8 Use of statistical methods

8.9 Evaluation and audit of quality

8.10 Actual state of quality assurance

9. Results

9.1 Measurement of results

9.2 Substantive results in quality, services, delivery, cost, profit, safety, environment

9.3 Intangible results

9.4 Achievement of results

10. Future Plans

10.1 Understanding of the current condition and concreteness of quality plans

10.2 Measures adopted to resolve shortcomings in the plan

10.3 Plans for further advances of company-wide quality control

10.4 Linkage with the long-term plans

Applicants for the Deming Prize submit an explanation report on the present situation of the company ("Jissetsu") along with their application to the Deming Prize Committee. The purpose of this report is to describe the applicant's current implementation status of company-wide quality control. Several different volumes of this report are required, each volume using the above checklist to describe the status of quality control in every major business area, including: corporate level, headquarters office, business divisions, sales offices, factories, research laboratories, et cetera. In smaller companies, some of these reports may be combined.

Application review process

The application and examination process has four steps: submission of the application form, submission of the explanation report, on-site inspection, and selection for the prize.

Each company applying for the Deming Prize must submit an application form to the Deming Prize Committee by November 20. When the committee receives the application, it makes a preliminary determination regarding the acceptability of the applicant. The applicant is then notified of the results by December 20.

After a company has passed the preliminary screening, it must submit an explanation report that describes the company's quality control practices and provides a prospectus of the company. This report must be written in Japanese and submitted by January 20. If the materials are approved by the Deming Prize Committee, then the applicant will be contacted to schedule an on-site inspection.

Two schedules are developed for the inspection. Schedule A is proposed by the applicant. This is the company's opportunity to put its best foot forward and identify those areas of strength that it wants the examination to assess. Schedule B is proposed by the JUSE examiners to probe for depth and breadth of quality deployment in areas not proposed by management in Schedule A. Schedule B is finalized by the committee after the company submits the Schedule A program. The Deming Prize Committee selects a subcommittee, whose composition is determined by the size and industry type of the applicant, to conduct the inspection under the guidance of a senior JUSE member.

After the on-site inspection, the subcommittee makes a recommendation to the Deming Prize Committee regarding the award of the prize to the applicant. The recipients of the Deming Prize are announced in October, almost eleven months after the application form was first submitted. In November, which is national quality month in Japan, the Deming Prize Committee recognizes those companies that have received the Deming Prize for that year. Each company that challenges the Deming Prize receives a feedback report, which summarizes the examiners' opinion of the applicant's quality control program.

For detailed information about the Deming Prize guidelines for Japanese or overseas companies, contact:

The Deming Prize Committee
Union of Japanese Scientists and Engineers (JUSE)
5-10-11 Sendagaya, Shibuya-ku
Tokyo 151 JAPAN
　Telephone:　03-5379-1227
　Telefax:　　03-3225-1813

The foundation for a quality journey

Challenging the Deming Prize is one way Japanese companies firmly establish the management of their business on sound quality practices and proclaim the assurance of their quality practices to their current and potential customers. To understand how Fuji Xerox responded to the attack by competitors in its home market, some background on the company is necessary.

In 1962, Fuji Xerox Company, Ltd. was established as a joint venture between Fuji Photo Film Company, Ltd. in Japan and Rank Xerox Company, Ltd. in England. The machines for the Japanese market were manufactured at the Iwatsuki Optics Company, Ltd., an affiliate company of Fuji Photo Film. Xerographic consumable parts were produced at the Takematsu factory of Fuji Photo Film. To expand the business, the Takematsu factory and Iwatsuki Optics Company were merged into Fuji Xerox in 1971, thereby consolidating production and marketing activities. Product teams in the United States would release their machine designs to Fuji Xerox manufacturing, which would then modify the designs to create the products Fuji Xerox would sell in Japan.

The Fuji Xerox pursuit of quality

Nobuo Shono, then a vice president at Fuji Xerox, decided to manage the new company using the principles of quality based on his prior experience with Fuji Photo Film, which had won the Deming Prize in 1956. In 1972, Shono started the "QC Movement" beginning with the engineering and production division because of his concern about merging the different cultures of the Iwatsuki and Takematsu factories with Fuji Xerox. He invited external coaches to Fuji Xerox to support the deployment of quality methods, particularly reliability methods and advanced statistical tools such as design of experiments. These coaches had two responsibilities: to provide instruction in the use of specific quality methods and to coach teams in the proper application of these methods. From 1972 to 1976, this coaching activity was focused on reducing Fuji Xerox quality problems in the Japanese market.

The team of external JUSE coaches began counseling in 1972 and continued through 1980. Professor Tetsuichi Asaka, an emeritus professor at the University of Tokyo, was the principal coach for Fuji Xerox, teaching business improvement methods. Dr. Genichi Taguchi, a professor at Aoyama University, taught and coached Fuji Xerox engineers in the area of robust statistical methods using design of experiments. Dr. Kenji Kurogane, a JUSE counselor, taught the "QC Story" method and its application in business situations. Professor Hajime Makabe of the Tokyo Institute of Technology joined the team in 1973 to teach and coach in reliability management and quality function deployment, a structured methodology for translating customer requirements into product designs. From 1972 to 1976, this team of counselors helped resolve problems with several products in the field. All of these efforts were directed only at the engineering and production departments; company-wide quality control had not yet been initiated.

The oil crisis of 1973 and the expiration of Xerox patents increased the cost-consciousness of Fuji Xerox. The Japanese market suffered from inflation, and businesses as a whole moved to cut unnecessary expenses. As a result, the volume of documents copied on leased machines decreased. In 1974, Fuji Xerox showed a decrease in profits for the first time since it was founded in 1962.

In 1975, Fuji Xerox worked to cut production expenses and increase its sales campaign to help counter the increased competition. These activities did not solve the problem.

In Japan, receiving the Deming Prize is evidence of a well-managed company. Companies that win the Deming Prize use that experience as a market advantage to inform their customers that their products meet higher standards of quality than others in the marketplace. In 1975, Ricoh became the first copier company to win the Deming Prize. It timed this award to coincide with the release of its DT-1200 model (the Savin 750 in the United States market). Because it had one-third of the parts of the competitive

Xerox machine and one-third of the weight, it cost much less to produce. Ricoh used the publicity from winning the Deming Prize to help launch this product. This was a considerable threat to the Japanese market of Fuji Xerox, but there were many other reasons that influenced the eventual Fuji Xerox decision to apply for the Deming Prize.

By 1976, Fuji Xerox senior management knew that it had to take more effective steps to counter the competition. It faced several challenges: provide the Japanese market with a product that would fully meet the special needs of reproducing kanji characters; reduce the energy operating costs through lower power consumption; increase the number of paper size options; and reduce the footprint of the machine for more compact office spaces. Atsushi Hirai, managing director of production, proposed to President Yotaro "Tony" Kobayashi that Fuji Xerox extend its QC practices to include the entire company. This proposal was accepted by the senior management team, and the activity was called the New Xerox Movement. Kobayashi became the principal leader. He established a New Xerox Movement Committee to develop the policies and direction for implementing Total Quality Control (TQC).

The policies (or objectives) established for the New Xerox Movement were:

- Deliver quality that satisfies customer expectations.

- Boost the quality control capabilities of sales and technology.

- Reduce the total cost of all business operations.

- Encourage greater personal creativity and innovation.

The action plan for deploying the New Xerox Movement relied on the use of the following QC methods to implement these policies:

- Manage using the Deming Plan-Do-Check-Act cycle.

- Manage by fact using data to characterize and understand processes and problems.

- Use What, When, Where, Who, Why, and How (referred to as the "5W1H") to describe problems.

- Act upon prioritized problems and improvements, focusing attention on the critical few activities.

- Prevent recurrence of problems.

- Promote the use of standards in products, processes, and services.

After the New Xerox Movement Committee developed the basic TQC policy and a deployment action plan, it was necessary to establish a firm foundation during the first year of the New Xerox Movement. The senior managers needed to understand TQC and to practice it in their own areas. They received training at a special TQC seminar. All officers, directors, and department managers were encouraged to discuss company-wide problems with their staffs and to create major action items for solving these problems based on these discussions. Each of the major problems identified was tackled by a team that was coached by the external JUSE counselors. From this effort, the timely development of competitive products targeted for the Japanese market was recognized as the highest priority for improving overall business performance.

Deployment of TQC within Fuji Xerox

The activities of the New Xerox Movement were promoted initially by the Business Affairs Improvement Office. The name of this group was changed to the New Xerox Movement Promotion Office in April 1977. (In most Western organizations this would be equivalent to the Corporate Quality Office.) The promotion office developed and deployed the internal communication campaign to expose employees to both the concepts of TQC and the improvement techniques that apply to each of the company's specific functional organizations. This office also provided education and training in TQC concepts and techniques. These activities raised company-wide awareness, understanding, and practice of TQC.

From April 1977 to October 1978, TQC deployment focused on four major activities: development of policy deployment and a senior management led Presidential Diagnosis to assess progress in quality deployment, development of Total Product Review, extension of QC Circles to autonomous improvement activity where teams had greater authority over their work process, and New Xerox Movement Conventions, which provided a means for sharing improvement successes.

Policy deployment

Policy deployment provided a direct connection between TQC activities and business activities. (The specific policies for the New Xerox Movement were identified earlier.) Policy is defined as a statement of management's desired direction or long-range objectives for the company. Typically, there will be three to five key business objectives or policies active within a Japanese company at a single time. Top management in Fuji Xerox began this long-range objectives planning for its 1978 annual plan during August and September of 1977. Consensus regarding the most significant problems facing the company and the direction of policies for the next fiscal year was established during a meeting of the senior management team during a night-long, off-site planning meeting. This overnight meeting is a method used by Fuji Xerox to focus the attention of the senior management team. It provides an opportunity for all senior managers to achieve alignment of their understanding of the business situation and to make joint decisions on the proper direction to be taken.

Presidential Diagnosis

In January 1978, a Presidential Diagnosis process was added to the policy deployment process. The purpose of the Presidential Diagnosis is to evaluate the progress for deployment of TQC activities across the business divisions and to share lessons learned from the line employees. Top management visits every workplace in each division to determine the degree of adherence to the quality policy, and to evaluate the strengths and weaknesses of the implementation. This also provides the workers with an opportunity to provide feedback to management about self-initiated improvement opportunities and for management to gather information about these improvements and share them with the rest of the company. As a side benefit, these visits by the senior management to the workplace improve morale and make it possible for management to make more decisions based on fact. The pilot for the Presidential Diagnosis was conducted under the direction of the team of external coaches in 1978 and became fully operational in January 1979.

Total product review

One focus of the TQC effort was to deliver attractive product quality and features to customers. The model 3500 copier was the Fuji Xerox answer to the Japanese market need. The TQC effort also served as the means for developing the Total Product Review. The Total Product Review was an assessment of major TQC activities in the product development process. In particular, it assessed the following areas:

- Evaluating the establishment of the quality assurance system throughout the new product development process ranging from product planning to development, production preparation, mass production, marketing, and service
- Encouraging the widespread application of statistical and analytical methods in the new product development process
- Improving the process for mass marketing and sales in support of the product development process and to improve the forecasting of sales targets by market segment

The first product to benefit from the Total Product Review was the 3500. The review was held in September 1978. The 3500 was the first copier that was developed completely by Fuji Xerox. It represented a significant improvement in copy quality reliability and cost over the prior product and met the Japanese customers' unique demands. Copy quality was improved to get excellent halftone reproduction of photograph originals, product reliability was doubled, machine cost was cut in half, time-to-market was cut in half, and the machine size was one-quarter that of the previous generation. Not only was the product a breakthrough, but so was the process used to deliver it to the market. For the first time, the quality methods taught by the Fuji Xerox JUSE coaches were used for product development: reliability management, design of experiments (Taguchi methods), as well as other problem-solving techniques, concurrent design practices involving production, service, and marketing. The challenge for the next phase of TQC was to take the lessons learned from the 3500 and expand them to other product developments and business areas.

Extension of QC Circle activity and New Xerox Movement conventions

The QC Movement had started in 1972 with a focus on improvements in manufacturing at the workstation level. This activity followed the model used at Fuji Photo Film and Iwatsuki Optics and was extended to the Ebina factory in 1973. The first QC Circle Convention was held in 1974 at Iwatsuki to provide an opportunity for recognizing the factory-based teams. In 1975, a three-factory joint meeting was held to encourage QC Circle deployment at the Takematsu factory. These team activities gradually spread throughout Fuji Xerox. With the development of the New Xerox Movement, the extension of QC Circles into other functional areas, such as the sales divisions, was encouraged. By 1978, the QC Circle Convention had been translated into a Xerox Circle Convention to encourage company-wide activities. A series of conferences was held throughout the summer to promote process improvement throughout the various areas: shop floor, production, management, sales, and design engineering. These conferences culminated in a Fuji Xerox convention in August 1978, which was held to share improvement ideas generated at the team level.

Throughout 1978, the activities of the company in developing management policy, accelerating product development, and extending the deployment of improvement teams had heightened the concentration on total quality. To maintain this momentum, Fuji Xerox announced to all employees, in October 1978, that the company was a candidate for the Deming Prize. The objective of this challenge was to provide a foundation for the decade of the 1980s. Indeed, the president's policy for 1979 was to continue the effort in total quality to attain the highest level of improvement while introducing new technology in products and service concepts that would make Fuji Xerox the leader in the information industry. This policy set the theme for the New Xerox Movement and the pursuit of the Deming Prize.

Challenging the Deming Prize

In November 1978, a committee had been formed to prepare for the challenge of applying for the Deming Prize. A New Xerox Movement Committee was appointed in June 1979 to provide senior management direction and oversight to the implementation of total quality. In addition, the New Xerox Movement Head Office was created by combining the New Xerox Promotion Office and the Quality Assurance Department, thereby fostering closer cooperation among activities and achieving an improvement in the deployment of the New Xerox policies.

During 1979, the Fuji Xerox improvement efforts were targeted toward the goal of winning the Deming Prize by strengthening the company's deployment of QC activities. This major work effort was added to the normal business operations of Fuji Xerox for the next eighteen months. Two activities formed the thrust of this effort.

First, the quality assurance system was strengthened. In 1979, a basic quality assurance policy directed toward making the business improvements necessary to become a strong candidate for the Deming Prize was established. The Presidential Diagnosis also helped to identify areas where the quality system needed improvement, and several improvements were made: improving policy deployment to include targets and means, conducting diagnosis at each phase of the product review process, reducing lead time for new product delivery, and managing further upstream for quality assurance in the product delivery process.

Second, work process improvement activity by QC Circles was greatly expanded. In 1978, a Xerox Quality Circle Sponsors Committee was formed to promote QC Circle activities. By the end of 1979, the number of active QC Circles had risen to 1006 and had spread from the factory level to the overseas operations of Fuji Xerox. In 1980, the Circle of Korea Xerox presented at the Xerox Circle Convention in Ebina. Another measure of active involvement of employees is the number of employee suggestions for work process improvement. In 1980, the number of employee-submitted improvement suggestions passed the 40,000-per-year mark. The pace of TQC activities at Fuji Xerox accelerated greatly with the encouragement from the Deming challenge.

In January 1980, Fuji Xerox began preparing for the preliminary examination conducted by the Deming Prize Committee. An explanation report was prepared to provide the current status of quality control as a basis for the examination. This report consisted of seventeen volumes and was submitted in April 1980. Each volume was fifty to eighty pages long; division directors and their staffs participated in the development of the volumes. Each volume was also reviewed by the New Xerox Movement Committee and the external TQ coaches. The development of this report helped to identify the areas that needed additional attention to improve the deployment of TQC across the various divisions in Fuji Xerox. This represented a massive work effort for both Fuji Xerox and the Deming Prize Committee examiners.

The following list describes the volumes, which represent over a thousand pages of material:

Volume 1	Corporate-Level
Volume 2	Headquarters Staff
Volume 3	Ebina Factory
Volume 4	Iwatsuki Factory
Volume 5	Takematsu Factory
Volumes 6-15	Sales Divisions
Volume 16	Xerox System Center
Volume 17	Glossary of Terms and Acronyms

Each volume was developed in response to the Deming Prize checklist and described the TQC activities and results in each department. In addition, each volume fully described one major improvement case. Overall editing was supervised by the New Xerox Movement Committee.

Fuji Xerox passed the preliminary examination of the Deming Prize Committee, and a site visit was scheduled for August 1980 (Schedule A) and September (Schedule B) to inspect the Fuji Xerox application of TQC. The inspection for Schedule A visit lasted three days and the inspection for Schedule B lasted two days. The Deming Prize Committee probed the depth to which the application of TQC had been accomplished throughout the organization. Some representative questions asked during the site visit included:

- Equipment rental is a distinctive feature of Fuji Xerox marketing. Has this marketing approach been deployed to its fullest extent?

- How is quality assurance maintained in the rental system?

- Has QC activity reached every part of the largest sales division?

- Is statistical quality control fully implemented in process rather than used merely for emphasizing process results?

- Over half of the Fuji Xerox employees are in sales divisions. What is the QC activity of the sales division? How does Fuji Xerox define excellence in a salesman?

- How does each new product development reflect input from the sales division?

- TQC is a philosophical revolution in business management. What is it in Fuji Xerox that was revolutionized?

The inspection process evaluated all aspects of the company's operation and uncovered additional areas where basic QC improvements could still be made. Nevertheless, when the results were announced on October 14, 1980, Fuji Xerox was awarded the Deming Prize.

To help understand the perspective of the New Xerox Movement and the role of the Fuji Xerox management in leading this effort, a portion of the corporate-level explanation report, which describes the commitment of senior management to continuing quality improvement, has been translated, summarized, and is reproduced in the following section.

Quality Statement by Fuji Xerox Leadership

This section is a consolidation of the individual statements prepared by the six managing directors of Fuji Xerox, which was included in their 1980 Explanation Report to the JUSE counselors in their Deming Application Prize. While the Deming Prize criteria do not require the same detailed description of leadership as the Baldrige Award or European Quality Award, this material provides an insight into the thinking of the senior management of Fuji Xerox as they were preparing to face the on-site examination by the JUSE counselors.

Since its inception in 1962, Fuji Xerox has experienced steady progress in its business improvement, both through the efforts of a vital work force and the encouragement of a supportive parent company. With the advantages of exclusive technology and patent protection, the company has achieved average annual sales increases of ninety-seven percent and profits of fifty-seven percent. This achievement was accomplished by offering a variety of high-quality products and developing domestic and international markets.

The economic winds shifted in 1973. Fueled by the oil crisis, the end of patent protection for specific technologies, and the introduction of superb competitive products into the market-place, the company business—which had reached its peak—

began to decline rapidly. By the end of fiscal 1975, Fuji Xerox had experienced a thirty percent decline in profit.

Faced with the biggest business crisis since the establishment of the company, Fuji Xerox managers had to take a hard look at reality. Although the economic climate triggered the situation, it was apparent that the true cause of demise was a fragile corporate structure.

Formed without the benefit of long-term direction during its rapid growth period, the Fuji Xerox infrastructure was wholly technological; it depended on the introduction of new technology without the challenging spirit of competition. And even though the work force was highly motivated to achieve company goals, they had poor cooperation skills. Meanwhile, management depended on high product sales for increasing revenue and profit while remaining neglectful of customer needs. Unfortunately, management's understanding of the actual state of the company was delayed because the company's flawed financial accounting reporting system masked many problems. Once the problems were identified, Fuji Xerox tried to reverse this crisis by reducing business volume. This resulted in short-term profit recovery, but neither market share decline nor profit decline was preventable in the long run.

After a great deal of deep reflection, Fuji Xerox came to realize its problems were the result of three main factors:

- An insufficient investigation of customer needs

- A dependency on exclusively acquired technology

- An employee mentality incapable of company-wide cooperation

Ultimately, a conclusion was reached: Improvement of the corporate structure would take priority over everything else. It was decided that corporate reform required the use of a rational and general approach based upon statistical techniques. In short, the facts had to be gathered and interpreted. This meant implementing a thorough approach to root cause analysis, and establishing a company-wide process for immediate communication of findings.

In 1976, Fuji Xerox introduced Total Quality Control (TQC) under the banner of the New Xerox Campaign. Through this effort, each employee became keenly aware of the importance of "Quality First," the value of interdepartmental cooperation, and the significance of incorporating quality at the source.

Initially, the focus was on the development of the best new products for the domestic copier/duplicator market. This approach included establishing a target for higher quality, and later, a goal to cut the traditional product development time in half. Previous products had been adapted for the Japanese market 'but were designed overseas. As a result of a renewed company-wide cooperative effort, the FX-3500—an epoch-making product in cost/performance ratio—was completed in May 1978. Since its launch, this model has enjoyed high praise from customers and has also made enormous contributions to business improvement. The success of the FX-3500 also influenced new product development in other business fields. The success of the FX-2080 engineering copier and the FX-485, both of which were produced with shortened cycle-times, are primary examples of the continuous improvement of this product line. In fact, the Fuji Xerox product development capability received praise from other Xerox companies, which helped to increase the confidence of the technical team and enhance the spirit of all employees. These products were the first Fuji Xerox products exported to other Xerox companies for sale.

The company's business performance improved from 1976 to 1979; sales and profit increased 1.7 and 2.2 times the 1976 level respectively. By internally funding these investments and thereby reducing outside capital requirements by half, the company raised the self-capital ratio approximately ten points to thirty-four percent, thus vastly improving its financial strength. Still, despite its growing success, the quality assurance system was inadequate and the lack of communication between organizations remained a barrier.

It is not easy for a corporation to force new trials on itself during a relatively trouble-free period, not to mention the difficulty faced in sustaining efforts to aim for even higher levels of performance. But failure to do so creates the opportunity for inattention and arrogance. In order to prevent setbacks in the corporate structure, Fuji Xerox saw a need to set up new, concentrated goals so that the enthusiasm and effort of every employee would be directed toward this great, ongoing challenge. It was this philosophy that led Fuji Xerox to apply for the Deming Prize.

To expand the quality policy and to provide stronger cooperation among all departments, qualitative and quantitative business fundamentals were clarified. Work was done to ensure that all employees understood the company's business objectives. And to further clarify the ultimate intent of TQC, corporate values and employee behavior models were clearly stated for company-wide distribution. Simultaneously, the announcement of the long-term business theme of "FX for quality," which targeted sales of 250 billion yen in 1983, was made.

Despite some initial internal anxiety, the company gained agreement and cooperation from the employees to enter the competition for the Deming Prize. Almost immediately thereafter, the company began to see changes in the way it did business. For example, improvements in the product development process made it possible to eliminate design defects at the trial production level, which was thus improved by reducing initial fluctuations through advanced control. As a result, the company's suppliers—who had represented seventy percent of the original production cost—were reduced from 254 to 145, while parts quality levels improved significantly. Additional results included active development of new products, expanded product distribution to overseas Xerox companies, and increased sales and profits.

During the challenge for the Deming Prize, there was a heightened understanding and increased use of statistical methods and management skills by the expansion of quality control (QC) circles in the factories, business departments, and main offices. In 1979, a company-wide quality problem-solving organization was formed with the Quality Assurance Department at its core. Cooperation among business, technology, and production was promoted, and this continues to be effective in solving chronic problems for current products. There were also diagnostic reviews conducted by top management and departmental heads. Various instructional seminars and educational activities were conducted. Steady progress has been observed in standardized measures of quality and cost reduction, as well as improvements in work processes.

The core ideology of Fuji Xerox is represented in the following policy statement for 1980:

> Fuji Xerox, on the foundation of internal and external trust, and with perseverance and innovation, will provide superior value, contributing to the promotion of understanding and harmony in human society.

The company believes that the future corporate environment will be characterized by increasing severity and change in the economic environment, as well as the continuous improvement of quality by its competitors. Thus, an active approach to the promotion of new technology development and new business areas must be pursued. This will be accomplished through the effective use of human resources and a more active exchange with the outside world. Continuing the effort to diligently internalize TQC concepts, without becoming complacent, is the only way to provide enduring excellent value, surpass others, and maintain the achievement of Fuji Xerox as a leading corporation in the Japanese information industry.

Future TQC improvements at Fuji Xerox will focus on the following activities:

- Promotion of multiorganizational trends at manufacturing locations and strengthening of cost quality.

- Promotion of centralized functions.

- Thorough implementation of resource conservation at the consumables plant and automation of the plant facility.

- Development of people who are capable of product planning with a global view, with an emphasis on participation in worldwide markets in cooperation with Xerox Corporation.

- Emphasis on fundamental technology and product development to meet the demands of the world market.

- Expansion of TQC to companies in cooperative relationships, including related Xerox companies, to make a contribution as a true leader in the information industry, and thereby increase the benefit of Fuji Xerox to society.

Continuing the Commitment

Today, the New Xerox Movement continues at Fuji Xerox with emphasis placed on continuing the improvement journey started by the Deming Prize challenge. Tony Kobayashi continues to guide Fuji Xerox in that journey.

Chapter Three
Charting the Course

In the latter half of the 1970s and the beginning of the 1980s, Xerox leaders recognized that the company would need to make significant changes in order to survive.

Senior management decided Xerox needed a unifying force or process, led from the top, in which all Xerox people would participate. This process, later named Leadership Through Quality, would focus on quality as the overriding principle for planning and executing work.

A note about the structure of this chapter. It follows the original outline of the Green Book: It begins with a definition of Leadership Through Quality and annual strategic goals for Xerox through 1987. These goals are followed by descriptions of the major elements of Leadership Through Quality that will make the year-by-year improvement possible: the use of standards and measurements; recognition and reward; communications; training; and organization structure and roles. The book outlines the implementation process for Leadership Through Quality; the resource requirements; the impact of senior management behavior and actions; and the decisions required to make Leadership Through Quality work. Xerox people continue to express amazement at the fact that the Green Book remains as relevant, vibrant, and fresh as it was in 1983. This is a tribute to its creators.

The Xerox Green Book documents the Leadership Through Quality strategy as created by the design Quality Improvement Team and agreed to by Xerox senior management, and outlines the year-by-year goals for implementation. This strategy has set the context for the implementation of Leadership Through Quality throughout the entire corporation. The strategy described in the Green Book is considered important; therefore, it has been given a full chapter in this book. The following is a synopsis of the Green Book.

INTRODUCTION

Leadership Through Quality is a goal, a strategy, and a process that will become the Xerox way of working at all levels of the corporation.

A **goal** - because it has not been achieved

A **strategy** - because it will provide a competitive edge and allow Xerox to attain business leadership through continuous pursuit of quality improvements

A **process** - because it will be a way of working. Quality is the fundamental business principle upon which Xerox management and work processes will be based.

The Xerox Quality Policy will be fulfilled by following the quality principles, practicing management actions and behavior of Leadership Through Quality, and using the quality tools.

The Xerox definition of quality:

- Meet customer requirements.

- Prevent errors rather than correct them at the end of the line.

- Instead of having an allowable level of defects, strive for error-free output.

- Instead of using indices as the principal measures, Leadership Through Quality relies on the cost of nonconformance to customer requirements.

Objectives of the quality policy:

- Instill quality as the basic business principle in Xerox, and ensure that quality improvement becomes the job of every Xerox employee.

- Ensure that Xerox people, individually and collectively, provide external and internal customers with innovative products and services that fully satisfy their existing and latent requirements.

- Establish management and work processes that enable all Xerox people to continuously pursue quality improvement in meeting customer requirements.

Required actions/conditions to meet the quality objectives:

- Supportive management practices that establish clear, consistent objectives and create an environment of openness, trust, respect, discipline, and patience.

- The continued use and expansion of competitive benchmarking and employee involvement.

- A process for identifying, agreeing to, and acting to meet customer requirements.

- A process for estimating and focusing on the cost of quality to achieve continuous improvement.

- Participative problem-solving using a common approach, statistics, and other tools.

- A pervasive commitment to do it right the first time.

Quality Improvement Process

To accomplish change, Xerox has developed the Quality Improvement Process and the Problem Solving Process. The nine-step Quality Improvement Process, or QIP, will be used by everyone in the company (see Figure 3.1). It will enable individuals and work groups to identify customer requirements; determine the standards and measurements to meet those requirements; and continuously evaluate and improve the quality of the work they perform and the output they deliver. In the early stages of Leadership Through Quality, every operating unit will apply the Quality Improvement Process to define its mission and agree on compatible objectives that equate to customer requirements. This will be part of the implementation planning process.

QIP elements:

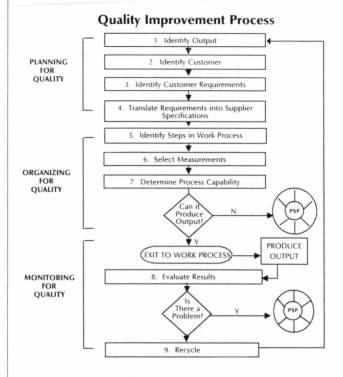

Figure 3.1: Quality Improvement Process Flowchart

- Identify units of work.

- Identify customers for the work.

- Identify requirements of the customers.

- Translate customer requirements into objectives and specifications to meet them.

- Identify steps in the work process to meet requirements.

- Select measurements for the critical steps in the process.

- Determine the capability of the process to deliver the expected outcome.

- Evaluate the results and identify steps for improving the process.

- Recycle for continuing improvement.

Problem Solving Process

The six-step Problem Solving Process (PSP) (see Figure 3.2) will enable analysis of a problem based on numerical data and other facts; the exploration of potential solutions; planning and implementing the best solution; and monitoring results until the objectives have been achieved.

Figure 3.2: Problem Solving Process

Cost of Quality

Understanding and using the concept of the Cost of Quality is an important part of the Quality Improvement Process. Xerox defines the Cost of Quality as the cost of nonconformance plus the cost of conformance to customer requirements. The Cost of Quality will be used in the context of Leadership Through Quality to create awareness, prioritize opportunities, and assess progress in all operating units or functions.

Implementation

Xerox will launch Leadership Through Quality through a structured and disciplined training process designed for all Xerox people. The training plan includes an orientation to develop awareness of the need for quality and the meaning of Leadership Through Quality; training and practice in the use and inspection of the processes; and training in tools and statistics that are part of the processes. Xerox will incorporate Leadership Through Quality principles in all of its new and existing training courses.

Communication is important to the implementation of Leadership Through Quality. Xerox people will be kept informed of overall corporate objectives in general and in their work group specifically.

ANNUAL STRATEGIC GOALS

To reinforce the long-term nature of Leadership Through Quality, specific annual strategic goals were set. These goals cover a five-year period (1983 through 1987). These goals will weave Leadership Through Quality into the existing company structure. Implementation will start with the units chosen by the Corporate Management Committee. The first-wave units are the Business Systems Group, Corporate Headquarters, Corporate Research, Office Products Division, Printing Systems Division, Rank Xerox Limited, Reprographics Business Group, Xerox Canada Inc., and Xerox Latin American Group. All other units will be included in wave two.

Through year-end 1983, the goals focus on communicating the start of Leadership Through Quality and emphasizing quality as a long-term business strategy. At the management level, Xerox will define the role of senior managers in implementing Leadership Through Quality. Corporate and operating management will communicate their unit's mission and objectives, and initiate their implementation plan. The goals (activities and desired results) for the remaining four years were:

1984 - Year of Awareness and Understanding

Activities:

- The training initiatives begun in the previous year continue: corporate operating committee members are trained and start to practice the QIP and PSP.

- Full training is completed for family groups chosen by the business units.

- Communications emphasize Leadership Through Quality, communicate business objectives, and continue to promote employee involvement and competitive benchmarking.

Results:

- Approximately 4000 middle and senior managers have been trained in Leadership Through Quality and are consistently using the processes associated with it.

- Trained managers are considered role models for their management practices.

- Customer satisfaction and employee feedback show improvement.

- All Xerox people begin to understand the dimension and scope of Leadership Through Quality.

1985 - Year of Transition and Transformation

Activities:

- All senior and middle managers are trained; training of first-line managers and supervisors is in place. In some areas, entire organizations are trained.

- Management development courses emphasize quality as the basic business principle in Xerox.

- Quality improvement goals become part of management objectives.

- Leadership Through Quality objectives are included in the 1986 operating plans and the 1985 long-range business plans.

- Quality is featured in Xerox external communications.

Results:

- Most Xerox managers (12,000 to 13,000) and approximately forty-five percent of individual workers (48,000) have been trained.

- Employee involvement, competitive benchmarking, and Leadership Through Quality are merged.

- Xerox people who practice quality improvement are rewarded and promoted, and become role models for others.

- The results of quality improvement become evident in customer awareness of the Xerox quality efforts, Xerox employees' increasing pride, and business results.

1986 - Year of Significant Results

Activities:

- Training of all remaining Xerox people is complete.

- All Xerox people understand their unit's quality and business objectives and have some quality improvement goals included in their work objectives and performance appraisals.

- An internal "Deming-type" award program is announced at the corporate level.

Results:

- Public recognition of Xerox as a quality company increases.

- Professional respect for Xerox management and work practices increases.

- Improving trends in Xerox market share, revenues, profit, and return on assets are established.

- Xerox products and services are beginning to become the industry standard in our primary businesses.

1987 - Year of Approaching Maturity

Activities:

- Implementation of Leadership Through Quality in Xerox is complete.

- Xerox people worldwide are applying Leadership Through Quality processes as part of their normal work.

- Goals and actions for continuing quality improvement are integrated in the planning, management, and review processes.

- Teamwork, discipline, and patience continue to develop as characteristics of the Xerox culture and work style.

- All appraisal, recognition, reward, and promotion systems are used routinely to encourage and reinforce continued quality improvement.

Results:

- Confidence in the corporation is widespread and consistent throughout all Xerox units and functions.

- The pursuit of quality improvement has become a way of life in Xerox.

- Xerox people are sharing in the benefits of Leadership Through Quality.

- Xerox management practices have become a world-class standard.

- Xerox and Leadership Through Quality become synonymous in the eyes of our employees, customers, suppliers, shareholders, and the general public.

- Xerox products and services are rated superior by our customers and industry analysts.

- The results of the Leadership Through Quality actions have made significant contributions toward the achievement of long-term corporate objectives.

- The tools and language of quality have become a cultural glue that binds Xerox people, everywhere.

- A behavioral shift—from aggression, attacking, and internal competition to supporting, sharing, and teamwork—has been accomplished.

STANDARDS AND MEASUREMENTS

Leadership Through Quality is intended to show that quality overrides all other considerations at Xerox. To achieve this, it is necessary to promote and maintain a work environment in which every behavior and action reinforce the basic business principle for Xerox. The standards and measures Xerox will use were chosen in this context and will be applied by Xerox people at all levels of the corporation.

Quality Improvement Process

The Quality Improvement Process will enable individuals and work groups to identify customer requirements, determine the standards and measurements to meet these requirements, and continuously evaluate and improve the quality of the work they perform. As issues or problems arise in the application of the QIP, the Problem Solving Process is used to enable a thorough analysis of the problem, the determination of the true cause, and the careful planning and implementation of the solution.

Cost of Quality is the single most dramatic measurement used to help Xerox people in the continuous improvement of quality.

Xerox will emphasize the use of the QIP rather than dwelling only on results. Consistent, effective use of the process will lead to the desired improvement in business results. As the implementation of the strategy progresses through the organization, family work groups and individuals who have been trained will get feedback on their use and application of the Quality Improvement and Problem Solving processes.

The standards and measures strategy will be integrated into business plans, operating plans, and annual objectives. Operating units are assigned to apply the QIP to define their mission and agree on compatible objectives that equate to customer requirements.

The involvement of all Xerox people is central to the standards and measurements strategy. The QIP will be used in all units and at every location and level in the organization so that quality becomes a way of life at Xerox.

Strategic guidelines

Achieving Leadership Through Quality requires changes in business and management processes, and increased attention to significant quality measurements. The strategic guidelines were developed to help units and individuals establish a quality improvement strategy. The guidelines fall into three groups: standards, measurements, and business process.

Standards include the guidelines describing the basic process and tools to improve quality and to set a standard of performance.

Measurements include the guidelines relating to quality measurements, and identify reduction of Cost of Quality as a key performance measurement.

Business process includes the guidelines to modify existing practices that complement the standards and measurement guidelines and are necessary to achieve continuous quality improvement.

Standards

"Standards" here refers to a statement describing a desired condition or state. Four process and performance standards will be used in pursuit of Leadership Through Quality: the Quality Improvement Process, the Problem Solving Process, statistical tools, and standards of measurement.

The Quality Improvement Process is designed to improve present work practices and processes. The Problem Solving Process is designed to eliminate current problems.

In the context of the QIP and PSP, Xerox people will apply statistical tools, including histograms, Pareto charts, fishbone (cause and effect) diagrams, and control charts.

Statistical tools are used to allow differentiation between common causes, which are linked to eighty-five percent of work problems, and special causes. Common causes are faults of the system and affect all members of a work group equally. Special causes are specific to an employee, machine, or work habit. They can be detected by statistical signals and can usually be identified and corrected by the individual. In other words, common causes are related to *effectiveness*—whether the organization is doing the right things. Special causes are related to *efficiency*—how well things are being done. To succeed, Xerox needs to solve both types of problems.

Benchmarking will be a standard process to evaluate the success of Xerox in meeting customer requirements. Each function should achieve and maintain superiority, or at least parity, in meeting requirements of customers in terms of quality, schedule, or cost performance.

Leadership Through Quality will be achieved by the primary strategy of meeting external customers' requirements. It will be a standard process for each unit to continually measure its performance in the marketplace relative to competition as determined by the customer. Each unit will establish competitive benchmarks for its major internal functions. The performance standard is to meet or exceed the best competitor's quality, schedule, and cost performance standard for each function.

Each unit will gather the necessary competitive data, establish a process to update the data, project the best competitor's future performance, and take the necessary actions to achieve and maintain competitive superiority. Progress should be measured and reviewed as a key item in operational reviews. Internal standards will be achieved through use of the Quality Improvement and Problem Solving processes. The result will be improved work, faster response, and lower cost performance.

Measurements

Quality improvement measurements will be applied to key indicators of performance at critical steps of the work process. The emphasis will be on error prevention and on doing things right the first time. Existing measurements will be reviewed and modified to be consistent with the Quality Improvement Process. Care will be taken to avoid the creation of unnecessary new measurements.

Measurable checkpoints should be established in the work process to permit the evaluation of the process, identify problems and actions required to improve probability of meeting objectives, and enable prevention of errors. The primary objectives of measurements are process control and defect prevention.

Cost of Quality will be used to build awareness of its impact on business results, and to help operating units prioritize opportunities for quality improvement and broadly assess progress. It is estimated that companies spend fifteen to twenty percent of their sales dollar on nonconformance; for Xerox, the cost of nonconformance is $1.8 billion. Two areas should be assessed in terms of Cost of Quality: individual components and the aggregate or total Cost of Quality, which is the sum of all individual components.

Individual components are opportunities for quality improvement; they will be used as measurements at critical steps of the work process. The aggregate will be used primarily to create awareness, prioritize opportunities, and broadly assess progress within an operating unit or function.

Cost of Quality will not be incorporated in financial measurement systems. Management will avoid using it for unit-to-unit and function-to-function comparisons. The main purpose of Cost of Quality is to track quality improvement progress for each unit or function. Application of the guideline for Cost of Quality will be left to the operating units. Units should identify vital few quality measures for each function to focus on the most important quality improvement areas.

Business Process

To achieve Leadership Through Quality, all elements of the standards and measurements strategy must be fully integrated into the business process. This integration will include, but will not be limited to, the strategic and long-range plan, the unit and corporate operating plans, all operating reviews, and the decision-making processes.

The role of managers will be to use, inspect, and improve the Quality Improvement Process. They must lead in the application of the process. Family groups and individuals will be evaluated for their consistent use and effective application of the QIP, PSP, and statistical tools.

RECOGNITION AND REWARD

Recognition is defined by Xerox as acknowledging, approving, or appreciating an activity or service. Forms of recognition include praise, personal thank you's, letters, mementos, dinners, and trips.

Reward, on the other hand, is the direct delivery of money or something with financial benefit; it includes pay, promotional increases, bonuses, and benefits (life insurance, health insurance, use of company cars, et cetera). Because people's actions and behaviors are instrumental in achieving Leadership Through Quality, it is necessary that recognition and reward systems support the goal. Existing and new reward systems should embody the basic principles in the mature state of Leadership Through Quality:

- The disciplined use of QIP and PSP is recognized and rewarded.

- Teamwork is encouraged by recognizing and rewarding all successful participants.

- Clear, specific quality improvement objectives will be included in performance appraisal and reward systems.

- Promotion criteria will include actions and activities that support the QIP and PSP.

- Effective use of competitive benchmarking and employee involvement will be recognized and rewarded.

- Recognition and reward programs will be evaluated to ensure they support the strategies. Where opportunities exist, new systems will be developed.

Guidelines for evaluating existing and proposed systems:

- Emphasize success rather than failure; stress positive reinforcement.

- Recognition and reward will be given as close in time to the event as possible.

- Recognition will be delivered in a more open, publicized way. When appropriate, reward will be delivered publicly.

- Clear recognition and reward criteria will be developed and communicated.

- Recognition and reward criteria will not only support the goal of Leadership Through Quality, but will also apply to other corporate policies and objectives, and will reinforce them as well.

Xerox will separate performance appraisal from annual salary reviews. The primary focus of appraisal will be recognition of both the accomplishment of results and the use of the Quality Improvement Process. The current Merit Increase Planning (MIP) system requires a prescribed distribution of appraisal results, which leads to stack ranking. This makes people feel like "numbers" and leads to competition within the group. Separating pay from appraisal allows managers to evaluate individual performance more constructively and eliminates competition. Performance appraisals will be separated from annual salary reviews by a minimum of three months. In conjunction with corporate personnel, existing appraisal systems will be examined for their suitability to achieve the objective appraisals described here. Where necessary, they will be modified.

Xerox will establish a bonus plan or plans so that Xerox people worldwide, where appropriate, can benefit from the long-term financial benefits that will result from Leadership Through Quality. Leadership Through Quality will provide financial benefits to Xerox, first from cost savings from work improvement, reducing cost of failure, and reducing costs of exceeding requirements. Later, benefits will result from increasing market competitiveness. To ensure ongoing commitment to Leadership Through Quality, Xerox people, where appropriate, will benefit from these financial improvements.

The format of the plan will be designed by compensation, personnel, and financial experts within Xerox. The plan must reflect and be consistent with the long-term health of the corporation. It must be tied to the objectives and accomplishments of the individual operating unit, must be understood by the people affected by the plan, and must be administered in a way that is perceived to be fair and equitable to the people within the unit.

COMMUNICATIONS

Success depends on consistent and credible communication. Formal communications, no matter how carefully worded or creatively crafted, will not succeed if they are at odds with management behavior. Every behavior and every action, particularly those of senior management, must reinforce the basic principles of Leadership Through Quality. Actions will be more important than words.

Some examples of actions include the following:

- Decision-making and problem-solving that follow principles of Leadership Through Quality.

- Recognition, reward, and promotion given to team players and people who exemplify the behavior of Leadership Through Quality.

- Insistence that each individual have a clear definition of the customer; a thorough understanding of the customer requirements; a complete agreement with the customer on what the requirements are and how they will be met; and the means and resources needed to meet those requirements.

- Visible and consistent signs that quality overrides all other considerations in deciding how Xerox behaves as an organization and at the individual level.

All of the Xerox efforts—training, reward and recognition, setting standards and measuring against them, decision-making, the way we treat the customer, and our quality focus—must send the same message: Xerox is a quality company.

Communication objectives

- Promote and communicate the Xerox Quality Policy to all employees.

- Explain why Xerox has embarked on Leadership Through Quality, and why successful implementation of it is key to the long-term success of Xerox.

- Explain what Leadership Through Quality is and what it will accomplish.

- Promote and encourage implementation of Leadership Through Quality.

- Portray and reinforce the value of continuous quality improvement.

- Reinforce the understanding, and encourage the use and inspection, of Leadership Through Quality by Xerox people at all levels.

- Describe expectations of Leadership Through Quality so they understand that this is a long-term program.

- Tailor communications to fit with the progress of Leadership Through Quality.

- Progressively influence the following to equate the name of Xerox with quality: employees, customers, suppliers, shareholders, the general public.

TRAINING

The Leadership Through Quality implementation strategy incorporates four ways of bringing about the desired changes and the realization of annual goals of Xerox as a total quality company. Training is one of the means to the end. It works in conjunction with the others: communications, recognition and reward, and standards and measurements. Training is designed to give Xerox people the knowledge and skills they need to continually improve the quality of their outputs—the products and services delivered to their external and internal customers.

Training is necessary when a requirement is identified for future performance that is different from what currently exists; and when this performance is dependent, at least in part, on additional knowledge and skills. For training to support that change, the knowledge and skill requirements must be identified. Then effective training programs must be designed and implemented.

Training objectives

- All Xerox people will be trained on the basics of quality.

- Training will be an integral part of the Leadership Through Quality implementation strategy.

- Training will be conducted in family groups (defined as a manager and his or her direct reports) so that work groups can learn and apply the appropriate skills together.

- Training will be tailored to level, function, and business area.

- Training will cover three major areas: the principles of quality, the tools and techniques required for total quality, and the management actions and behaviors needed to make quality a reality in the work environment.

- Training will be tailored to the individual operating unit.

- Training content and design will be grounded on core concepts and processes that are applicable to all Xerox people.

- Training will use instructional methods and delivery approaches (including advanced learning technology) appropriate to the level and needs of those being trained.

- Training must facilitate the transfer of skills and knowledge taught to the actual work environment of the family group. Feedback and evaluation mechanisms will be built into all training to ensure effectiveness.

- Training must be reinforced. Refresher courses will be designed and used after the initial training cycle has been completed.

The core modules for training will cover five areas:

- Orientation: To create awareness of the need for a total quality process in Xerox.

- Family group startup: To begin formal Leadership Through Quality training in a family group environment, under the direction of the family group manager.

- Knowledge and skill training: Two components—all will be trained on the Quality Improvement Process, which includes the Problem Solving Process and statistical tools. Second, all managers will be trained on managing quality. This training will provide managers with the skills they need to manage quality improvement and to prepare them for their roles as family group managers, trainers, and group facilitators.

- Specialized technical skills: Provides additional tools and advanced techniques to those who will need them to continually improve the quality of their work. Design engineers, for example, will learn how to design and evaluate experiments.

- Initial quality improvement project: On-the-job application of the Quality Improvement Process to one or more of the family group's units of work, designed to reinforce newly acquired knowledge and skills.

Operating units will supplement the core modules to meet their specific functional and business needs.

Leadership Through Quality will be implemented tops-down in family groups. Each family group manager will be responsible for the development of the knowledge and skills of his or her subordinates and the subsequent application in the work environment of what has been learned. People at all levels will have the benefit of role models and examples to guide them in the change of their own behavior.

Managers will be responsible for all four major training implementation activities in Leadership Through Quality training: Learn-Use-Teach-Inspect (LUTI). The manager first learns the concepts and skills in his or her family group, then applies them in the work environment. Then the manager participates in subordinate training, perhaps assisted by a quality specialist. Finally, the manager inspects the use of concepts and skills by employees in their environment. It is the manager's role to inspect how the family group uses the process, not the results. The manager acts as a coach and does not judge performance results.

An orientation will be available in December 1983 that will allow the Board of Directors to understand the key elements and implications of Leadership Through Quality strategies and implementation plans.

Members of the Quality Implementation Team form the initial core of quality specialists and will take responsibility for the training and support of this management group. Executives and general managers will be divided into family groups, which follow the organizational structure as closely as possible. The initial group will be the Corporate Operating Committee, extended to include the heads of all the first-wave units. The unit quality officers will participate in, and support, this program.

Unit heads will then lead their own senior staffs in the same program, supported by their quality officer and Quality Training Task Force member. This training will occur approximately three months after that of the Corporate Operating Committee.

Implementation of Leadership Through Quality will be supported by quality specialists within the operating units. These specialists will deliver training and provide consultation to family groups and family group managers.

The Quality Training Task Force will design, pilot, and produce materials for the core modules of Leadership Through Quality training based on requirements of the Quality Implementation Team. Internal and external consultants will be used. The emphasis on teamwork and family groups implies a strong bias within the training toward interactive group activities, rather than mass or individualized training approaches. However, some of the basic skill components, such as statistics, do lend themselves to an individualized format, using delivery mechanisms such as interactive video discs or computer-aided instruction. These approaches will be researched.

Operating units will establish a training plan consistent with objectives and guidelines specified in this document. Operating units will develop implementation plans that are consistent with the corporate-wide guidelines and tailored to their mission and business environment.

ORGANIZATION STRUCTURE AND ROLES

The organizational structure supporting Leadership Through Quality includes the creation of a Corporate Quality Office under the direction of the corporate vice president of quality, reporting to the corporate chief staff officer, and individual quality offices in the major operating units under the direction of an operating unit quality officer who reports to the operating unit head.

Each major operating unit in the first wave has appointed a quality officer who reports directly to the operating unit head. These officers will also have a dotted-line reporting relationship to the corporate vice president of quality. Within each operating unit, the quality officer will assemble an operating unit Quality Implementation Team responsible for Leadership Through Quality training, employee involvement, benchmarking, communications linked to Leadership Through Quality, and appointing implementation team members, reporting to each major function in the operating unit.

Roles and responsibilities

There are four key functions in the implementation strategy: the operating unit head, operating unit senior staff, operating unit quality officer, and generic functions performed by the operating unit quality specialists.

The role of the operating unit head is to lead by example: to use the Leadership Through Quality principles and tools, and to incorporate Leadership Through Quality strategies into operating plans.

Operating unit senior management should manage according to Leadership Through Quality and support its use throughout the unit. Management should be role models for employees and should monitor the progress of Leadership Through Quality implementation.

The operating unit quality officer should help the unit design the process and strategy for Leadership Through Quality implementation. The officer also should help establish objectives, standards and measurements, and ensure the use of the Quality Improvement Process and the Problem Solving Process.

Generic functions performed by the operating unit quality specialists include acting as subject matter experts on the tools, methods, and processes of Leadership Through Quality; helping managers to plan the implementation and training for Leadership Through Quality; supporting managers in development of quality objectives, and standards and measurements; facilitating quality improvement projects; and providing the means to measure the effectiveness of Leadership Through Quality training.

Corporate Quality Office

Although the primary achievement of quality improvement will occur in the individual operating units, corporate senior management has a key role in initiating, supporting, and sustaining the operating unit activities. Senior management must also implement approaches at the corporate level which, in their own right, will lead to quality improvement.

The corporate vice president of quality heads the Corporate Quality Office and is charged with providing leadership and a unifying focus on the quality improvement effort. The Corporate Quality Office will provide the umbrella for coordinating all aspects of quality, including competitive benchmarking, employee involvement, and quality improvement tools and technology.

The Corporate Quality Office is responsible for developing the process for the implementation of Leadership Through Quality and for monitoring progress toward the achievement of this corporate goal. It will keep the Corporate Management Committee and the operating units regularly informed on plans and progress.

The Corporate Quality Office exists in both a narrow and broad sense. In its narrow sense, it will have the following functions: implementation support, strategy planning, project coordination, quality technology, and competitive benchmarking. The office also will work closely with Corporate Personnel in communications, training, and employee involvement.

In its broad sense, the Corporate Quality Office also consists of the Quality Implementation Team and the Quality Training Task Force. Many of the functions of the Corporate Quality Office can only be fulfilled if the office is understood in this wider context.

Leadership Through Quality Network

A Leadership Through Quality Network will be established in the fourth quarter of 1983. It will consist of the Corporate Quality Office, the operating unit quality officers, and appropriate specialists as determined by the corporate vice president of quality. The network will help facilitate an ongoing functional relationship between the Corporate Quality Office and the unit quality officers after the Quality Implementation Team completes its work.

IMPLEMENTATION

Implementation of Leadership Through Quality will be a continuous process. Guidelines for implementation have been developed for the areas of training, recognition and reward, standards and measurements, and communications. An organization structure has been designed to manage the overall implementation. First-wave units will now begin to develop their specific implementation guidelines.

Nine operating units were selected for the first wave of implementation; members from those units have formed the Quality Implementation Team. Between August and December 1983, individual members of the team will divide their time between initiating implementation in the operating units and designing and participating in the corporate pilot training program.

Because the first-wave operating units vary in terms of size, geography, and organizational structure, some operating units may implement Leadership Through Quality in subunits following a wave strategy similar to that used in the corporate implementation. Others may implement the unit all at once.

RESOURCE REQUIREMENTS AND FINANCIAL IMPLICATIONS

The implementation strategy makes extensive use of training for all Xerox people worldwide. A tops-down training strategy is being incorporated to reinforce the role model of senior management and to provide consistency for the implementation. The resource requirements at the corporate level reflect the tops-down training strategy and the need for ongoing promotion of the Leadership Through Quality effort.

Most of the resources are required at the operating unit level, where implementation takes place. As each unit prepares its implementation plan, these resources will be identified. A set of guidelines to assist the units in identifying these requirements is included.

Centralized costs

The centralized investment in training occurs in 1983 and 1984, although ongoing maintenance costs for the core modules are required. In 1983, these costs are associated with the development of the core modules and the pilot training of the quality officers. The training of the Corporate Operating Committee will occur in 1984.

Centralized costs are also identified for indoctrination of wave-two quality officers and expenses of the Corporate Quality Office in supporting Leadership Through Quality at the corporate level. All other costs associated with the implementation of Leadership Through Quality will be the responsibility of the operating units.

Operating unit resources

Creation of the unit implementation plans and identification of resource requirements are the responsibility of the operating unit head, with the assistance of the unit quality officer. The unit quality officer is responsible for making the necessary recommendations in terms of resource requirements and associated trade-offs.

Some examples of resources that could be required by operating units include: salaries and associated expenses of quality officers, specialists, training management and administrative support; costs associated with the Unit Quality Implementation Team and the preparation of the units' implementation plans; and expenses related to an expanded communications effort.

SENIOR MANAGEMENT BEHAVIOR AND ACTIONS

The implementation of Leadership Through Quality requires significant support and initiative from managers at all levels of the corporation. The changes involve a redefinition of management responsibilities. Leadership Through Quality is not expected to change traditional managerial authorities and accountability. Decision-making, planning, organizing, communicating, leading, and evaluating performance are roles that belong with the manager. Leadership Through Quality will strengthen the role of the manager as a teacher and leader who will establish work processes in the work group that are in line with the principles of Leadership Through Quality.

Traditionally, the role of a manager has been to establish a system, direct work through subordinates, make assignments, develop a rationale for setting standards and performance goals, evaluate the people and their work, and provide further training for poor performers or replace them.

Experience has shown that there are better ways to achieve the same objectives. Perhaps more importantly, these other approaches seem to reduce the inherently adversarial relationships that are created between manager and subordinate in the more traditional management style.

In these approaches, the manager's traditional role is expanded to include the following:

- Provide consistency, clarity, and continuity of purpose for the organization based on meeting customer requirements for the work product of his or her group.

- Seek more creative ways to involve people in solving the problems they face in pursuit of their goals.

- Assure that the processes and solutions being implemented are cost-effective.

- Assume responsibility for continually improving the system in which subordinates perform their tasks.

- Ensure that the people within the organization practice the Quality Improvement and Problem Solving processes; monitor their effort; make suggestions; assist the implementation; and evaluate improvements.

- Ensure that subordinates receive training and reinforcement in elementary statistics and other analytic tools needed to monitor performance of their activities.

- Act as a role model in these same skills by learning and then using them.

Leadership Through Quality has a very different view of the managerial role. It requires the manager to develop a set of skills and practices to become a coach and facilitator of the process by which subordinates, acting as a team and knowing their customer requirements, proceed to perform their tasks.

In order for this type of change to take place, managers must recognize several key premises:

- Managers will set standards that fully meet customer requirements.

- The techniques for reviewing objectives and variance from plan are in the Quality Improvement Process. Emphasis is placed on "how" and "why" as well as "what."

- Problems are primarily with the system, not with the workers. Understanding this will reduce the adversarial relations, enabling subordinates to speak freely, without fear, and with a feeling that management, while accountable for the business, can be influenced.

- Improved performance can only be achieved by constantly removing the performance barriers in the system or by finding the creative breakthroughs to new systems for improving work and performance.

- The subordinates are most able to help improve the system. Recognizing this will help promote teamwork.

DECISIONS REQUIRED

The Leadership Through Quality strategy developed by the Quality Implementation Team is based on a number of principles that will dictate behavior and action at all levels of management. They are designed to foster the leadership of people and the management of processes in order to bring about improved business results.

The decisions required are framed as recommendations. They have been developed through a process of consultation with unit management. The senior management team must examine them carefully in order to decide whether they are prepared to do the following:

- Commit themselves and their organizations to the principles, actions, and behaviors described.

- Fulfill their responsibilities for implementation.

- Practice the processes indicated.

Epilogue to the Green Book

Time has proven the Green Book to be a remarkable document. Ten years after its creation it continues to guide and provide the framework for a continuing TQM effort throughout Xerox. Also remarkable is the fact that the vast majority of the elements described in this strategy were actually implemented on a global basis across 100,000 people in over 100 countries.

Chapter Four
Continuing on the Journey

Legislation creating the Malcolm Baldrige National Quality Award was signed into law on August 20, 1987. The purpose of the award is to help improve the quality and productivity of United States businesses by:

- Helping to stimulate American companies to improve quality and productivity for the pride of recognition, while obtaining a competitive edge through increased profits.

- Recognizing the achievements of those companies that improve the quality of their goods and services, and providing an example to others.

- Establishing guidelines and criteria that can be used by business, industry, government, and other organizations in evaluating their own quality improvement efforts.

- Providing specific guidance for other American organizations by publishing detailed information on how winning organizations were able to change their cultures and achieve eminence.

The award is named for Malcolm Baldrige, who served as Secretary of Commerce from 1981 until his death in 1987. In his honor, the award recognizes the contribution of managerial excellence to long-term improvement of business efficiency and effectiveness.

Award criteria

The award criteria are based on the following key quality concepts:

- Quality is defined by the customer.

- Businesses' senior leaders must create clear quality values and build them into the way the company operates.

- Quality achievement results from well-designed and well-executed systems and processes.

- Continuous improvement should be a factor in the management of all systems and processes.

- Companies need to develop goals, as well as strategic and operational plans, to achieve quality leadership.

- Shortening the response time of all operations and processes should be an objective of the quality improvement effort.

- Operations and decisions of the company must be based upon facts and data.

- All employees should be suitably trained, developed, and involved in quality activities.

- Design quality and defect and error prevention should be major elements of the quality system.

- Companies need to communicate quality requirements to suppliers and work to elevate supplier quality performance.

Members of the Board of Examiners for the Malcolm Baldrige National Quality Award examine a company's application to assess the company's level of quality performance. The award examination is based upon criteria that represent the highest levels of overall quality and business competitiveness. The examination criteria address seven categories that represent the major components in a quality management system. These categories are further divided into examination items for scoring. The award criteria are subject to continuous improvement by the Board of Examiners and change from year to year. Although the seven major categories have stayed the same since 1988, the examination items and their descriptions have been improved with each year's experience in the award process. When reviewing an application, it is necessary to understand the specific criteria that were used for that year.

The 1989 Malcolm Baldrige National Quality Award criteria included twenty-seven examination items. The following list shows the seven categories of criteria and their supporting examination items:

1. Leadership
   1.1 Senior management
   1.2 Quality values
   1.3 Management system
   1.4 Public responsibility

2. Information and Analysis
   2.1 Scope of data and information
   2.2 Data management
   2.3 Analysis and use of data for decision-making

3. Planning for Quality
   3.1 Planning process
   3.2 Plans for quality leadership

4. Human Resource Utilization
   4.1 Management
   4.2 Employee involvement
   4.3 Quality education and training
   4.4 Employee recognition
   4.5 Quality of work life

5. Quality Assurance of Products and Services
   5.1 Design and introduction of products and services
   5.2 Operation of processes
   5.3 Measurements and standards
   5.4 Audit
   5.5 Documentation
   5.6 Quality assurance of operations and business processes
   5.7 Quality assurance of external providers of goods and services

6. Quality Results
   6.1 Quality of products and services
   6.2 Quality and business process quality improvement
   6.3 Quality improvement applications

7. Customer Satisfaction
   7.1 Knowledge of customer requirements and expectations
   7.2 Customer relationship management
   7.3 Customer satisfaction methods of measurement and results

The detailed description of each examination item is contained in the application guidelines and is described as a set of areas to address. These areas to address are evaluated and scored by the Board of Examiners. The examiners consider key business factors and the environment specific to each award applicant within the context of its respective industry. Examination items are scored by the Board of Examiners using the following three evaluation dimensions:

1. Approach -   the methods used to achieve the purpose of the examination item.

2. Deployment - the extent to which the approaches are applied to all relevant areas.

3. Results -   the outcomes and effects in achieving the purposes of the examination items.

Application review process

The application review process begins with the first-stage review, in which a team of examiners is assigned to review each submitted application report. Examiners' assignments are based on their areas of expertise. Examiners are thoroughly screened to eliminate any potential conflicts of interest and are trained to reduce variability in scoring. The examiners independently evaluate the application, using the Baldrige Scoring System and Evaluation Criteria as their guides.

A panel of judges reviews the examiner teams' collective scores and selects the applications that will be evaluated during the second-stage review. In the second-stage review, a consensus assessment of the independent examiners is facilitated by a senior examiner who is assigned to head up the team. The panel of judges reviews the scoring and assessment comments to verify that the evaluation process is being followed, and determines whether an applicant should receive a site visit. If an applicant is selected for a site visit, a team of examiners, including significant representation from the consensus team, conducts the assessment. During the site visit, examiners clarify and verify the information contained in the application. Under the guidance of a team leader, the site visit report is submitted by the team of examiners for consideration by the judges. The judges evaluate the relative merits of the finalists and select recipients of the award based on their assessment of the company's ability to serve as a national role model of quality excellence. Each applicant for the Malcolm Baldrige National Quality Award receives a detailed feedback report from the judges, which describes the observed strengths and areas for improvement of the applicant's quality processes.

For detailed information about the current Baldrige Award application guidelines and assessment procedures, contact:

> Malcolm Baldrige National Quality Award Office
> National Institute of Standards and Technology
> Route 270 and Quince Orchard Road
> Administration Building, Room A537
> Gaithersburg, MD 20899
> Telephone: (301) 975-2036
> Telefax: (301) 948-3716

Xerox application process

In late 1988, the Xerox senior management team decided to prepare an application for the 1989 Baldrige Award. They did not decide, at that point in time, whether they would use the application solely for self-assessment of their progress in implementing Leadership Through Quality or whether they would submit the application to compete for the award. It was decided that the Business Products and Systems segment of Xerox Corporation, representing 52,000 U.S. based employees, would be the organization to develop the application.

The Xerox application development strategy was to focus on the long-term improvement aspects of the company's quality efforts and to involve a significant number of its people. Senior management selected a team of twenty people from functional areas throughout the company to develop the application. These team members were chosen because they could provide expertise related to the seven award categories. The individuals selected for the team were deliberately not chosen from the ranks of quality professionals. Most were selected on the basis of their demonstrated use of Leadership Through Quality as line managers. On average, each team member was a mid-level manager with twenty years of Xerox experience.

The team represented all functional areas of the Company. In addition, executive-level sponsors had responsibility for each of the major categories. The corporate executive staff (CEO, president, and executive vice presidents) worked closely with the Xerox National Quality Award (NQA) Team throughout the four-month application development process.

Developing the Application

The NQA Team first met on January 3, 1989, to develop its strategy. The approach taken by Xerox in preparing for the NQA challenge reflected the TQM approach it had embraced in 1983. Xerox faced this challenge in the same way that it had come to face all challenges: organize a team, develop a strategy, use quality tools for analysis, involve line managers, provide incentives for motivation, allow the team's progress to be self-driven, involve all supporting employees through awareness, and build communications.

Team members established a February 22 deadline for the first draft of the application. Some of their initial activities included:

- Brainstorming potential responses, by category, and identifying strengths and weaknesses of the Xerox quality system.

- Benchmarking companies that had completed Baldrige applications in the prior year: Digital Equipment Corporation, Hewlett-Packard, IBM, Milliken, Motorola, and Westinghouse Nuclear Fuel Division.

- Establishing roles and responsibilities for the team: category coordinators, executive sponsors, and editors.

- Assigning data-gathering responsibilities.

- Establishing category teams to develop the Xerox response to each of the seven Baldrige categories.

The first draft of the application, which was approximately 300 pages, lacked integration between the categories and sections. An editorial review board was formed to integrate all the responses to the categories and to serve as a final voice for issues that were cross-category, because a tendency to collect data without responding to the specific requirements of the criteria was noted. The first draft was written without all of the input from the organization, but it served as a vehicle for a structured solicitation of feedback from the functional organizations.

The second draft was completed March 17. An internal assessment of the application was conducted by three trained Baldrige examiners. The application began to take shape as information between categories was integrated. The executive sponsors and coordinators from the team coordinated the response for each category and set the strategic structure for the response. A major discovery was that, like most problem-solving entities, Xerox people had become comfortable with discussing what was wrong or what went wrong. They were not prepared to tout what they did well.

The third draft, which was completed April 8, included the feedback from the internal examiners' assessment and the editorial review board's revisions. By now, the line managers who would face the examiners were fully engaged and had come to recognize the pressure of their responsibility in the NQA application process. Weekends were spent seeking facts, exploring data trails, and gathering evidence to support results. Senior management reviewed this draft to decide whether the application should be submitted for the award or only used internally for the intensification of Leadership Through Quality. After that decision on April 14 to submit the application, the team finished editing the application to meet the seventy-five-page limit. The application report was submitted May 1. Early on, the team had established an operating guideline that each statement in the application would be backed up with proof statements, data, or examples. The team gathered the supporting evidence and created, at the completion of the project, approximately 225 notebooks of backup data. This data was cross-referenced to the application subjects to support the statements made in the application. The people who would answer the examiner's questions had to know where the data was and be able to retrieve the information. Data was managed by a central librarian for each of the seven category response teams. The information would serve as proof statements and support for responses to questions during the site visit.

During the course of the application development, David Kearns made numerous visits to encourage the team, conduct interviews with the application team members and the category response teams to support their information requirements, and to understand their strategy for developing the document. During the four-month period, each of the Xerox executive vice presidents who would participate in the examination worked with the team to provide input.

The NQA Team members received significant recognition for their efforts even before the results of the examination were known. At the completion of the site visit, a team social event was held to recognize the efforts required for preparing the application. This recognition was not dependent upon the performance of Xerox during the site visit; it recognized the team for its stimulation of company-wide interest in the award process and the completion of the application development and follow-up phases. All that remained was to await the judgment from the Board of Examiners.

The anticipation ended on November 21, 1989, when Xerox people were told that Xerox Business Products and Services and Milliken were the 1989 Baldrige Award winners. Following the presentation of the Baldrige Award to Xerox, management of Business Products and Services (United States Marketing Group and Development and Manufacturing) publicly acknowledged the contribution of all employees through a series of recognition events. Kearns and Allaire hosted a dinner for the NQA Team members and their spouses. All of the Xerox corporate officers, including Yotaro "Tony" Kobayashi, attended. Each team member received a Steuben crystal sculpture of an eagle, representing the team's soaring contributions to Xerox. The celebrations at all Xerox locations were spontaneous and genuine. People felt good. Each employee also received an additional day of vacation in 1990 to recognize their support of quality and cumulative accomplishments of Team Xerox. Mixed with these good feelings was the growing sense of responsibility to live up to the standard of the award, which was bestowed upon Xerox.

Enablers of success

The success of the Xerox application process effort was the result of four key process enablers: executive involvement; category sponsors; the teamwork of the NQA Team, which was supported by Team Xerox; and the reliance on the tools and methods of Leadership Through Quality. These enablers provided the organizational framework for developing a strong Xerox application.

Application summary

The entire 1989 Xerox application for the Malcolm Baldrige National Quality Award has been reprinted separately. It is available from Xerox— see the details provided at the end of the book. The following section reproduces the Leadership category response and summarizes the major points made in the remainder of the Xerox Baldrige application.

1.0 Leadership

Xerox senior managers personally drive continuous quality improvement.

David Kearns, Xerox' Chairman of the Board of Directors and Chief Executive Officer, with his senior executives has been the driving force in every stage of Xerox' total quality control strategy, **Leadership Through Quality**. It was senior management who first recognized the need for a total quality thrust at Xerox, who developed the initial plans, who benchmarked Xerox against other leading world-class companies, who embarked on TQC strategies, and who became influential role models in creating a long-term sustained environment in which Leadership Through Quality could grow.

A significant influence in Kearns' decision was his personal observation of the performance of Fuji Xerox, our joint venture in Asia. Beginning in 1976, Fuji Xerox had used TQC to completely turn around slipping performance, becoming such a quality success story that in 1980 they were awarded the Deming Prize.

Concurrently, Senior Vice President of Manufacturing and Engineering Frank Pipp began to benchmark Xerox performance against world-class companies, primarily the Japanese. He found that our 8% per year productivity improvement lagged far behind the eighteen percent per year we needed to reach parity in five years. Our production costs were comparable to our competitors' selling prices, and it took us twice as long to introduce new products as it took them. In addition, competitive product quality was about twice as good.

In September, 1982, the Corporate Management Committee, led by Kearns, reviewed and approved the concept of a total quality process for Xerox. In early 1983, twenty-five senior Xerox managers enthusiastically reached consensus and commitment to the specific objectives and content of the Xerox quality effort. This was the way the business would be managed in the 1980's, the 1990's, and beyond.

Senior management documented policy, objectives, and the desired future state of the company in a briefing book. In April 1983, Kearns appointed a corporate vice president of quality; a Quality Implementation Team comprised of senior managers from the major operating groups, divisions and corporate headquarters; and a supporting Quality Training Task Force. For six months both teams worked with the management of each unit, the Corporate office, and other senior executives to develop plans for implementing the Leadership Through Quality strategy. The result was the core document from which operating unit strategies and plans are developed and implemented.

In addition to our Japanese competitors, we benchmarked major U.S. multinational companies for philosophy, top management involvement, training, culture, attitudes, roles, implementation strategy, resources and other key elements of TQC.

Kearns and his staff acted as role models by being the first group to be trained. Kearns then led the training of the senior management team. Their training included modules on interpersonal skills for group work, the concepts of internal and external customer/supplier requirements, Cost of Quality (COQ), awareness of statistical process control, and systematic problem-solving and quality-improvement processes—all of which would become key factors as Leadership Through Quality spread throughout the company.

Training proceeded through the company by "family groups," which are natural groupings of employees and managers as defined by the requirements of the job. Senior executives, after spending a week in intensive quality training, then spent another week conducting the training of their direct reports, assisted by a professional trainer. After the training, the manager guided the family group in the use of the quality processes. This "cascaded" training and quality responsibility spread Leadership Through Quality throughout Xerox from the top down; it also ensured the ongoing participation of managers at all levels.

Kearns and his direct reports participated in quality-improvement projects as part of their training, just like other family groups. They initially completed two projects that were of high priority: one to improve the effectiveness of the Corporate Management Committee meetings, and the other to streamline the quarterly operations reviews held with the operating units. Both projects required use of the nine-step Quality Improvement Process (QIP) and the six-step Problem Solving Process (PSP), two key aspects of Leadership Through Quality (described in Item 2.3.1). The resulting process improvements are still in use.

Kearns, Xerox President Paul Allaire, and other senior executives also enriched their knowledge of TQC through discussion and consultation with quality experts, including W. Edwards Deming, J.M. Juran, Genichi Taguchi and Philip Crosby.

We continually assess our growth. In 1987 Kearns and Allaire commissioned an independent assessment of the company's quality plans and progress. They devoted a great deal of time and personal effort to analyzing assessment results and to the development of corrective actions for improvement. Resulting direct actions included: (1) the affirmation of Customer Satisfaction as our number one priority; (2) development of a team strategy to achieve this number one priority; (3) a greater focus on senior management leadership, which led to the creation of role model standards and personal action agreements; (4) guidelines for annual unit assessments; and (5) managerial training in inspection of the use of the quality processes. **"Inspection"** as used at Xerox means focusing on the steps used to accomplish results. Our inspection emphasis is on managerial coaching in the effective use of the quality processes and skills to prevent defects and achieve continuous improvement.

Senior executives personally lead top-level quality improvement teams focused on projects relevant to their areas. Examples include: the use of COQ to assist in prioritizing projects; the use of competitive benchmarking to establish clear models for each department; the development of a "customer obsession" strategy (described in Item 7.2.1); the use of quality tools in Partnership operations reviews (the Xerox concept of "Partnerships" is explained in Items 4.2.1 and 7.2.1); the upgrading of senior management role modeling and inspection of the use of quality processes; and the use of recognition and reward to reinforce application of quality processes.

Senior management further demonstrates commitment to quality at various recognition events. For example, either Kearns or Allaire have participated in every "Teamwork Day," Xerox' annual bi-coastal recognition of excellent quality improvement teams, since the inception of Teamwork Day in 1983. Teamwork Days are major events and are attended by thousands.

The president and his senior executives take the lead in communicating the Corporate quality vision throughout the company.

After Paul Allaire became president in 1987, he initiated quarterly videos to communicate directly to all Xerox employees. These are effective for reinforcing the quality and customer satisfaction messages.

Allaire also visits Xerox' major geographic locations in the first quarter of each year to conduct "state of the company" meetings. Included is a reaffirmation of the Quality Policy and of the company's vision for continuous quality improvement. These meetings are participative, encouraging questions from the audience. In February 1989, Allaire and Wayland Hicks, Executive Vice President for Marketing and Customer Relations, "met" with 45 sales District personnel live-via-satellite from Headquarters in Stamford, Connecticut. The company's quality values and priorities played a significant part in their presentation and were further explored through call-in questions from the audience.

Kearns takes every opportunity to reinforce Leadership Through Quality throughout the company at recognition events, executive meetings, and facilities visits, as well as through interviews in internal publications and videotapes.

More than 95% of all employees have completed core training in Leadership Through Quality. The first segment of their training includes a video of Kearns describing the company's quality vision, quality policy, and strategy for implementing TQC.

Xerox leadership leaves no doubt that customer satisfaction is our number one priority, or that use of TQC is the strategy for achieving that priority. The 1989 Priority List communicated by Allaire once again reinforces Xerox' priorities: (1) Customer Satisfaction, (2) ROA, and (3) Market Share.

The annual report is perhaps the company's strongest external vehicle for widely presenting objectives and priorities to our shareholders. Xerox has chosen to deliver a single message on the covers of our annual reports for 1987 and 1988: "Customer Satisfaction is the key to our success."

Senior executives consider customers, employees and suppliers to be critical contributors to the success of Leadership Through Quality. For this reason, senior management actively encourages continuous contact with these groups. Following are some examples:

Production employees in manufacturing areas are represented by the Amalgamated Clothing and Textile Workers Union (ACTWU). The company and this enlightened union have worked together to bring everyone into the quality process, with Allaire, Kearns and top-ranking union officials taking the lead. This unique partnership with our represented employees is fostered in many ways. For example, in 1982 a union official was part of one of the first company-sponsored benchmarking teams to visit Japan. A senior union official is one of the speakers at annual Teamwork Days. The ACTWU/Xerox relationship is further highlighted in Item 4.2.1.

Contact with customers is facilitated by the Focus Executive Program, in which senior executives are each assigned one or two Major Account customers. "Major Accounts" are companies that have large-scale business relationships with Xerox. These executives serve as advocates or "champions" within Xerox for these customers. They meet with "their" customers often to thoroughly understand the customers' requirements and expectations of Xerox. Approximately 270 Major Accounts are currently part of the program.

Suppliers are a vital and integral part of the Xerox team. Vice presidents with direct product responsibility frequently work with suppliers, considering them as much a part of the operation as their own employees. In a support area, Vice President Norton Rosner led a team of Xerox and Honeywell people in the successful improvement of control systems procurement, using the Xerox Quality Improvement Process. Suppliers also participate in reviews and in employee events such as Teamwork Days. (Supplier relationships are discussed in Item 5.7.1.)

Senior executives have been active in delivering the Leadership Through Quality message outside the company. Audiences have included customers, competitors, government agencies, educational institutions, and nonprofit community organizations.

Following is a sampling from the last two years:

- David Kearns, an early advocate of a National Quality Award, was a member of the White House Conference on Productivity. Kearns was a speaker at the ASQC National Quality Forum in 1987; he will serve as chairman of this event in 1989.

- Kearns has delivered the message of quality to many organizations, including the Washington Economic Club; the Universities of Vermont and Texas; North Carolina State University (with Governor Hunt); the AT&T Senior Management Forum; Columbia Graduate School of Business; U.S. Department of Labor; U.S. Department of Transportation; and Harvard Business School.

- Recognizing that business must play a lead role in improving the quality of our educational process, Kearns has co-authored, with a leading educator, Winning the Brain Race, a book outlining a bold plan to make our schools competitive.

- Paul Allaire's external speeches include addressing the Annual Labor Management Conference sponsored by the Departments of Commerce and Labor; the Massachusetts Special Commission on Quality Improvement; and business schools including Dartmouth, Carnegie Mellon, and Utah State University.

Quality exchanges also occur frequently between Xerox, often represented by senior executives, and other companies. We have shared our Leadership Through Quality program with, among others, Florida Power and Light, Hewlett-Packard, Texas Instruments, Corning, Motorola, IBM, Westinghouse, and Milliken. Our senior executives continue their involvement in sustaining excellence at Xerox.

Leadership Through Quality was introduced to all Xerox employees in the Fall 1983 issue of *Xerox World*, the quarterly Corporate magazine. David Kearns, then Xerox President, defined our quality strategy, policy, and processes and explained how each employee could begin to support them. He stated:

"Leadership Through Quality may very well be the most significant strategy that Xerox has ever embarked on. It is aimed at fundamentally changing the culture of Xerox over the next several years. Leadership Through Quality calls for moving from an ambiguous understanding of customer requirements to a systematic approach for understanding and satisfying those requirements; from accepting a certain margin of error followed by corrective action to doing things right the first time; and from unstructured and individualistic problem solving and decision making to predominantly participative and disciplined problem solving and decision making."

This introduction went on to state the quality policy and objectives and to summarize the plans for implementation.

Leadership Through Quality: A Total Quality Process for Xerox documents the complete framework. This 92-page "greenbook," the key reference document for management, thoroughly describes the interaction of employee involvement, competitive benchmarking, and quality tools—the three pillars of Leadership Through Quality

Training and reference materials have been developed and disseminated to fully communicate how quality values are to be achieved. The initial documentation consisted of seven volumes totaling 586 pages. Today, the U.S. Marketing Group catalogs 93 items in their Leadership Through Quality library. A small sample is shown in Figure 1.2.1-1.

Title of Media	Format	Description
Leadership Through Quality Interactive Skills Workshop (Flex training workbook)	87 pages, spiral bound	Discusses interactive skills behaviors; assessing, reassessing; discussion guides include troubleshooting; boundary problems; coding and discussion worksheets.
Leadership Through Quality Measures of Quality Tools for understanding and inspecting processes	114 Pages 3 ring binder	Measures of Quality is a 3 day
Leadership Through Quality IAS flipchart pads	2' x wall chart	
Leadership Through Quality Quality Restaurant	Video Casse (1/2"	

At the foundation of Leadership Through Quality is the Xerox Quality Policy. It simply and clearly communicates our expectations to customers, shareholders and employees. It states:

XEROX QUALITY POLICY

Xerox is a quality company. Quality is the basic business principle for Xerox. Quality means providing our external and internal customers with innovative products and services that fully satisfy their requirements. Quality improvement is the job of every Xerox employee.

The framework for each Operating Group to establish quality objectives is provided by the Xerox Corporate Philosophy reproduced in Figure 1.2.1-2.

XEROX CORPORATE PHILOSOPHY

We succeed through satisfied customers.

We aspire to excellence in all that we do.

We require premium return on assets.

We use technology to develop product leadership.

We value our employees.

We behave responsibly as a corporate citizen.

Xerox quality values are continually reinforced by direct management communication. *Xerox World* has focused on Leadership Through Quality topics in 23 articles in the 19 issues published since 1983. Three covers have spotlighted quality themes.

Agenda, a journal for Xerox managers, has featured one of the members of the Corporate Office discussing Leadership Through Quality in eight of the 12 issues since 1983.

The management behaviors necessary to support changing Xerox' culture were initially described in the greenbook. They have become an integral part of the assessment and development of managers, as described in Item 1.3.1.

To support the self-improvement process, each year managers survey their employees to receive feedback on personal management style and behavior. A data base is maintained to enable individuals and organizations to assess progress. Figure 1.2.1-3 reflects the continuous improvement in the answers to the three key survey questions for the composite of managers' scores in the Development and Manufacturing Group (D&M). The high rating also has a high index of agreement, indicating that most or all employees definitely feel their manager demonstrates Leadership Through Quality.

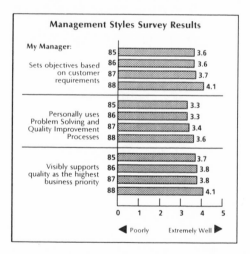

Additionally, assessments of the overall progress in implementing Leadership Through Quality are carried out using the annual Employee Satisfaction Measurement System. Each Operating Group structures questions into modules to measure the critical ownership factors in its area of the business.

Formal management assessment of the implementation of Leadership Through Quality within each Operating Group is conducted annually by the Quality Offices and reviewed by group presidents.

The principles of Leadership Through Quality guide all of our business decisions and directions; this is consistent with making customer satisfaction our number one priority. For example:

- 1986 - Manufacturing employees empowered to stop the line to prevent defects.

- 1987 - $30 million incrementally expended to ensure product quality of the 1065 copier prior to launch.

- 1988 - Customer service level improved despite reduced profit level.

- 1988 - One thousand new employees at the Webster manufacturing facility—a 30% increase—trained in Leadership Through Quality.

- 1988 - Sales Districts received expanded authority in pricing, delivery, collection and credit to respond immediately to customer needs.

The Corporate values have been fully deployed through each operating unit and at every level. A key part of the initial Leadership Through Quality implementation is the development of family group mission statements consistent with the total quality objectives and processes. Group missions and objectives are reaffirmed each year, consistent with Corporate priorities as described in Item 1.3.1.

The development of leaders who own and practice Xerox quality values is ensured through management replacement planning, which requires our senior managers to qualify as "role models" against standards set for management behavior. These standards are being deployed through all management levels.

Paul Allaire, in his 1989 priorities for quality, challenged each Xerox unit to compete for the national quality award in their home country, or if none exists, to lobby their government to establish one. This will provide the leadership to sustain quality levels that will be the benchmark for our industry in the 1990's.

At Xerox the principal means for integration of quality values into day-to-day management of operations is the objectives cascade process. That process starts with the Xerox Quality Policy and extends to the individual performance objectives of all salaried employees. Hourly employees are, of course, a critical link in the Leadership Through Quality process, and since 1980 their contracts have included a clause that covers joint union/ management support of quality objectives. The 1989 contract specifically supports continuous quality improvement (see Item 4.1.1).

To help focus and quantify continuous quality improvement, William Lowe, Executive Vice President in charge of Development and Manufacturing, has recently committed his organization to annual improvements which will result in achieving the following aggressive objectives by 1993:

- Benchmark schedule performance;

- 50% Unit Manufacturing Cost reduction;

- Four-fold improvement in reliability.

Objectives focusing on customer satisfaction and on continuous quality improvement are developed annually between salaried employees and their managers.

These objectives are based on Xerox' policy, philosophy, and priorities, which cascade throughout the company, becoming more specific at each successive level. Following is an example of this quality deployment cascading from the CEO to a forward product program buyer:

1) Xerox Philosophy and Priority:

- We succeed through satisfied customers.

- We aspire to excellence in all that we do.

- Customer satisfaction is our number one priority.

2) Business Products and Systems priorities:

- Increase customer satisfaction levels in order to achieve a competitive advantage with our customers by implementing plans which improve product and business process performance, simplify doing business with Xerox, and enable our people to fully meet customer needs at the point of contact.

- Increase the effectiveness of our Product Delivery Process to achieve quality, cost and delivery targets. Integrate the Customer Delivery Process and Product Delivery Process to ensure quality product launches that meet customers' needs (see Item 5.1.1).

- Provide personal leadership and effective support which empower Xerox people to do what is right for our customers and achieve our business objectives.

3) Development and Manufacturing objectives:

- Develop and deliver quality products and support services that fully satisfy customer requirements. External: Assure customer requirements are systematically built into new programs and strategies through the development cycle. Internal: Deliver products at the planned launch date, at the targeted customer satisfaction performance, and at approved cost levels. Continue the implementation and integration of the elements of Leadership Through Quality into the day-to-day business processes.

- Develop and implement business and product strategies based on customer requirements.

4) Business unit objectives:

- Achieve product quality, cost and delivery targets.

- Achieve specific customer satisfaction targets: Sum of significant problems and percent satisfied.

- Achieve Leadership Through Quality: Managers as role models, competitive benchmarking, COQ, and Employee Involvement.

5) Chief Engineer objectives:

- Achieve customer satisfaction targets.

- Utilize phase gate inspection checkpoints and criteria for customer satisfaction defined by the Product Delivery Process.

- Review Customer Satisfaction Measurement System (CSMS) results, targets, and actions at department reviews and communications meetings.

- Establish customer or user group partnerships for duration of Product Delivery Process.

- Provide supplier status and customer appraisal of status at reviews.

6) Manufacturing Resource Team objectives:

- Implement and maintain a quality philosophy and system that yields target achievement and process improvement.

- Achieve specific product quality targets.

- Demonstrate improvement in the use of quality processes.

7) Forward product program buyer objectives:

- Use the Material Acquisition Process and Continuous Supplier Involvement to assure the required performance of procured material.

- Assure that parts quality plans are available for each part sourced.

- Use only Commodity Team recommended suppliers (see Item 5.7.1).

This cascade helps ensure customer satisfaction through continuous quality improvement, which is defined as the job of all Xerox employees.

Managers play four vital roles in enabling their subordinates to accomplish continuous quality improvement: (1) Managers help individuals set objectives focused on quality; (2) Managers act as role models for employees; (3) Managers coach employees in behaviors and practices that contribute to TQC; and (4) Managers act as resources for Quality Improvement Teams (QITs) working on quality-improvement projects.

Paul Allaire, working with the Corporate Quality Implementation Team, developed and issued three guideline documents:

- "Standards Present In Exemplar Organizations That Manage For Quality"

- "Standards For A Management Process"

- "Model Leadership Through Quality Agreement"

These guidelines define continuous quality improvement responsibilities and expectations for all levels of management.

Xerox' "Standards for a Role Model Manager: Leadership Through Quality" provides behavior criteria for all levels of management (see Figure 1.3.1-1).

STANDARDS FOR A ROLE MODEL MANAGER
LEADERSHIP THROUGH QUALITY

1. Visibly demonstrates support and promotion of the Leadership Through Quality strategy.

2. Personally uses, and encourages others to use, the processes and tools including Problem Solving, the Quality Improvement Process, Competitive Benchmarking, and Cost of Quality in all key business areas.

3. Uses customer satisfaction as a key measure in all business decisions and assures that unit activities result in an improvement in customer satisfaction.

4. Encourages formal feedback from peers, superiors, and customers on personal management behavior, and uses the feedback to modify personal style and behavior as appropriate.

5. Establishes the expectations and requirements for the Quality Plan, its implementation plan, the measurements, and the inspection process. Communicates to reinforce progress consistent with these expectations. Meets the goals set.

6. Hires and promotes people who actively practice the principles of Leadership Through Quality and works to help develop and broaden them. Counsels and instructs those who are deficient to advance them toward the role model standard necessary for promotion.

7. Recognizes and rewards the actions of individuals and teams effectively utilizing Leadership Through Quality to achieve improved business results.

8. Through regular inspections, identifies individual and team weaknesses and provides coaching and guidance in the use of the quality processes to improve.

In accordance with Kearns' direction, we are not counting or specifically budgeting (as a line item) for quality. Kearns' directive is "invest as appropriate, don't count it, and no cost reductions should impact it." While competitive cost pressure and ROA objectives have driven cost reductions across all areas of the business, Xerox' commitment to Leadership Through Quality is demonstrated by continued investment in the quality process.

A major resource allocation to the quality process is the Quality Network, which consists of individuals who have specific full-time or part-time specialized quality responsibilities. These activities include acting as consultants to managers, facilitators for QITs, and trainers and communicators of quality. The network includes over 900 employees contributing 400 man-years of effort, for any given year.

We estimate that over the last four years, Xerox has invested over $125 million in Leadership Through Quality training (see Item 4.3.1).

An example of resource allocation to our total quality process is the annual department, group and Corporate Teamwork Days, which showcase employee QITs. These events provide an exciting forum for demonstration of employee involvement, quality processes, and results. Outstanding teams are selected to participate, and all employees are encouraged to attend.

Inspection—in the Xerox use of the term—is an integral part of our Leadership Through Quality process: LUTI, a key process element, stands for Learn-Use-Teach-Inspect. We inspect for progress towards integration of quality values into our management processes. These inspections include audits by our Corporate Audit organization, annual assessments by quality officers, ongoing operations reviews, annual objectives performance evaluations, and surveys.

Managers are inspected and evaluated on Leadership Through Quality criteria, which are part of their annual performance appraisals.

A key inspection is the quarterly Customer Satisfaction Improvement (CSI) meeting, in which senior managers review customer satisfaction data from our external customers. These data are collected by our Customer Satisfaction Measurement System (see Item 7.3.1). The meetings provide a forum for senior management to inspect the top problems impacting customer satisfaction; to identify actions to resolve and prevent recurrence; and to review strategic issues which have been focused by what our customers tell us. All of our internal processes, programs, audits, inspections, or surveys ultimately take second place to the point of the CSI meetings: Quality is what the customer says it is.

Corrective actions for units not achieving quality plans come in many different forms. Self-help, other Xerox units, and outside consultants are used, depending on the situation.

Self-help generally takes the form of the six-step PSP and/or the nine-step QIP. With either approach, the objective is to identify root causes of the problem and then work towards a solution using Employee Involvement (EI).

Often, similar problems have been encountered and overcome by other Xerox units. In those instances, information sharing is used to build on past experiences. Our employees are eager to share with each other their problems, solutions, and work processes.

If internal correction resources are not available, we engage outside experts. We have used consulting firms, universities, and individuals as the situation requires.

An example of continuous improvement is the Managers Guide for the Xerox Account Management Process. The guide details a consistent, comprehensive account management process for sales which focuses on understanding and satisfying customer requirements. Both the process and the guide were developed by a QIT and are currently being implemented.

Managing for quality is a constantly improving process, changing as our customers' needs change, and improving as we upgrade processes to meet those needs. Inspection is the primary tool for identifying a need for process improvement actions, followed by groups' employing the QIP and PSP to fill voids, fix problems, and continually seek out improvement opportunities.

A frequently used tool for quality process improvement is the final agenda item for many meetings—the meeting evaluation. Each meeting attendee provides comments on process items that he or she believes were well handled in the meeting and those that were not. The meeting scribe records all comments. This activity provides a process focus for all attendees to use in subsequent meetings: Continue to build on the positives and strive to prevent the negatives.

The quality management process is improved by employees' learning better ways to do their jobs. Refresher training supplemented by new training programs is available to all employees. Many of these programs respond directly to needs identified by employees as they encounter barriers in their work.

Senior management creates and maintains close cooperation among functions by: (1) acting as role models, and (2) establishing and participating in cross-functional management processes. The following partial listing of cross-functional management processes is described in detail in other categories of this application (as shown in parentheses):

• Business Resource Management Statement (3.1.1).

• Customer Satisfaction Work Process (7.2.6).

• Quality Implementation Team (1.3.2).

• Employee Involvement Teams (4.1.1).

• Product Delivery Process (5.1.1).

• Customer Delivery Process (5.1.1).

• District Partnerships (1.3.2).

To foster the close cooperation across functions necessary to reach our quality goals, Xerox created the Quality Implementation Team. Headed by Vice President of Corporate Quality Norman Rickard, the Quality Implementation Team is an ongoing council comprised of senior quality representatives from each of the major operating departments and functions. The Quality Implementation Team has been operating since the introduction of Leadership Through Quality. Meeting quarterly as a total team, they review the status of each unit; check on progress towards goals; and develop recommendations for long- and short-range quality targets. This is a forum for cross-pollinating the best quality approaches across the company.

The U.S. Marketing Group's (USMG) "District Partnerships" strategy is an example of a cross-functional team approach to quality and customer satisfaction improvement. The strategy developed from the work of two different QITs, using the quality process: the Administrative Practices team, working on improving administrative and business processes; and the Vendor of Choice team, working on identifying customer perceptions and on meeting customer requirements. Working independently, both teams identified a need for an increased focus on the customer.

That recommendation led to the creation of our District Partnerships. A Partnership is a close, cross-functional team of sales, service, administrative, and business managers who share common goals, including profit-and-loss responsibility. They are empowered to take the actions needed to improve performance and provide customer satisfaction, and are measured on their team performance as a "partnership."

Similar Partnerships exist at the Regional and Operations Group levels, with vice-presidential-level people as managing partners. After the Partnerships were tested and proven, they were expanded to all districts.

Other cross-functional QITs are assembled to attack specific needs. A recent example of a team comprised of representatives from several major functions was the group that developed a worldwide Third-party Sales Program.

Annual "Team Excellence" awards are given in recognition of use of the QIP to achieve outstanding results. QITs with far-reaching corporate impact generally include multifunctional and international representation.

The theme *Team Xerox* expresses the importance of cross-functional activities aimed at customer satisfaction. This message, prominently displayed in letterheads, television advertising, and internal and external publications, has been sent consistently to our employees and to those outside the company.

A further aid in fostering cooperation across functions or departments is the Xerox Quality Policy, which defines quality as "fully meeting customer requirements, both internal and external." Every employee receives mandatory training in the uses of the PSP and QIP, which both teach the concept that the person receiving your output is your customer. This internal customer has requirements that the team member, as a supplier, must satisfy. Almost always, each employee is both a supplier and a customer, with mutual obligations: As a supplier, an employee must satisfy customer requirements; as a customer, he or she must clearly identify what is needed. Many departments use surveys to measure the level of internal customer satisfaction.

The most important indicator of improved cross-functional integration—as with every aspect of quality improvement—is the satisfaction of our customers. Our favorable trend in customer satisfaction is discussed in Item 7.3.2.

The key strategy for integrating disparate units—whether they are departments within the same function or geographical sites thousands of miles apart—is the universality of Leadership Through Quality training, practices, and principles. This common approach encourages the formation of cross-functional teams to attack business issues which could not be as effectively addressed by either unit alone. The indicator of improved integration for these teams is simple: Have they achieved measurable results that impact customer satisfaction?

One example: A Field Operations QIT in El Segundo, California, addressed lagging sales of a sophisticated printing system. Sales and software personnel together designed a computer-based modular training upgrade which gave sales representatives a much better understanding of how to present the printing system to customers in terms of what the customer needed the system to do. This cooperation led to dramatically improved product sales—to 150% of target. The training created by the integrated team has now been shared with, and is being used by, Xerox Canada, Inc. and Rank Xerox.

This QIT won a Xerox Team Excellence Award in 1988. This cross-functional success story is not an isolated incident. It is representative of the Xerox trend toward increased cooperation across functions in pursuit of our quality goals

Those quality goals are not confined to Xerox' U.S. operations. Quality training materials have been translated into various languages and are used at all Xerox sites. Our European affiliates in Britain, France and Holland also embarked on the TQC path using Leadership Through Quality. They have been honored as recipients of the British Quality Award, French Quality Award, and the Dutch Quality Award. This testifies to the universal effectiveness of Leadership Through Quality.

The company has been generous in sharing its quality knowledge with others. Early in the implementation of Leadership Through Quality, many organizations came to headquarters to discuss our approach. By the latter half of 1987, the number of requests had increased to the point that one day a month is set aside as Corporate Quality Day. Customers, suppliers, academic and government organizations spend a full day reviewing our quality initiatives and their results. Kearns, Allaire, or other senior executives are personally part of the program so that the executive attendees can directly discuss the critical senior leadership role.

Forty-nine organizations attended Quality Day at the Stamford Headquarters in 1988. A sampling includes AT&T; General Electric; Proctor & Gamble; Texas Instruments; Lehigh, Tennessee, and Rutgers Universities; the U.S. Department of Defense; the Federal Quality Institute Task Force; and the U.S. Postal Service.

Numerous other visiting organizations go directly to activity sites to benchmark functional areas such as Information Management, Manufacturing, Engineering, Human Resources Management, and Distribution.

In 1983 Xerox began an aggressive supplier quality training program; we were subsequently awarded Purchasing magazine's Quality Award. Suppliers are trained in statistical quality control and given implementation support at no cost to them. Other U.S. companies, in addition to Xerox, are the beneficiaries of Xerox-trained suppliers' improved products and services. K.G. Seitz, Vice President of Seitz Corp., wrote Xerox, "What impresses me most about Xerox is the commitment, not only to produce a quality product, but the corporate decision to dedicate a vast amount of internal resources to train their vendors in exciting quality programs. Total quality has taught us how to work together as a 'Team' with our number one objective 'Satisfy the Customer'.

"Thanks to Xerox, our company was not only able to achieve excellent status with Xerox with 100% quality, but we have used our quality techniques with companies like IBM, Wang, Data Products and Texas Instruments." (Quality techniques taught to suppliers are covered in more detail in Item 5.7.1.)

Because we recognize that the company's annual report is a major vehicle for communicating with our stockholders, quality and customer satisfaction coverage are substantial and are highlighted as "the key to our success."

When the Tri-State United Way Campaign Committee, located in Connecticut, expressed concern about its effectiveness, Xerox stepped in to provide committee members with quality training in group interaction, meeting facilitation, and use of the quality improvement processes. The committee reported increased effectiveness after their training.

Xerox encourages its people's involvement in outside quality-related activities. The Chairman of the Board of the American Society for Quality Control is Doug Ekings, a Xerox executive whose activities are fully supported by the company. Xerox is represented as a charter member of the Quality Council of The Conference Board.

Xerox employees are chairpersons and active members of National and International Standards consortiums. Their work includes such complex challenges as developing a standard document and data processing system, and developing a single standard computer language. Some of these consortia are part of the U.S. Governments' National Institute of Standards and Technology (NIST), and American National Standards Institute (ANSI).

Other senior executives are very active in promoting quality. In 1988 Richard Palermo, Senior Vice President U.S. Marketing, gave TQC presentations to more than 2,000 people in nonprofit organizations ranging from Alfred University to the American Hospital Association.

Xerox was selected as a recipient of the "Performance Through People" award given by *Incentive* magazine. This award was given in recognition of Xerox' demonstrated philosophy that "customers, employees, and management are all inextricably linked" to improve products and services. Only five American companies were selected to receive this award. The January 1989 issue of *Incentive* further identifies Xerox as a model for working to improve profits "through customer satisfaction and employee dedication."

For the past five years, Xerox has participated in an executive-exchange program with government agencies. Government executives work in the Xerox Corporate Quality Office to learn about the Leadership Through Quality approach to TQC. At the end of the year's assignment, these executives become a nucleus for growth of total quality in the government. Agency representatives include people from the Department of Transportation, the U.S. Post Office, Housing and Urban Development, and the General Accounting Office.

The Xerox Customer Systems Division has sent an exchange executive to the U.S. Department of Defense to work specifically with the DOD on the use of TQC. He also went with members of the DOD to Japan as part of a benchmarking visit to study Japanese quality methods. This is one example of Xerox participation.

Employees are encouraged to become involved in community activities, many of which focus on health, safety and the environment. The Xerox Social Service Leave Program grants employees of absence at full pay to work in a variety of community-service projects of their choice. More than 350 employees have participated in this unique program.

A sample of 1989 leave grants include:

• Improving quality of life for cancer patients and families.

• Developing a model program of options for caring for the aged.

• Training disadvantaged youth to hold better jobs.

At our two major U.S. manufacturing sites, Webster and El Segundo, medical, chemical, and fire response personnel and equipment are available as backup or supplemental support to community resources. This Xerox help has been used by both communities.

A statement from Kearns encapsulates Xerox' worldwide environmental protection policy: "Xerox Corporation is committed to the health and safety of our employees, products, customers, neighbors, and the environment. Economics is no excuse for not complying with this policy. If we cannot afford to follow it, we will get out of the business."

Xerox is environmentally responsible; the company's goal is to ensure that every Xerox operating unit complies with or exceeds all generally recognized standards and legal requirements in every area of environmental protection and waste management. Specifically, the objectives of the Xerox policy for its operations are to ensure that: (1) emissions are controlled within levels posing no threat to public health and welfare; (2) wastewater discharge quality is controlled at levels designed to maintain the chemical, physical and biological integrity of the receiving sewage facilities; and (3) disposal of hazardous liquid and solid waste material is conducted in a manner designed to promote the protection of health and the environment and to conserve valuable material and resources. Where no generally recognized standards exist or apply, Xerox follows a policy of "good practice."

Of its own accord, Xerox launched a worldwide environmental

safety assessment of all its facilities in 1985. Its purpose is to assure that all Xerox locations and operations are environmenally sound.

The company uses a systematic process to evalute any facility activities, past or present, that may affect the environment. If problems are identified, we promptly notify public authorities, and then either implement remedial projects or recommend further investigation to gain a better understanding of potential problems.

Xerox continues to allocate funding for such voluntary environmental-protection projects even while we seek to reduce general overhead costs.

Our quality objectives for health, safety and environment are promoted both inside and outside the company. Our environmental health and safety organization has done special toxicity research on materials used in our products. The results of those activities have been published to the scientific community and appropriate government agencies to make the information available for developing safe exposure standards for industry and the community. Xerox led the way in the establishment of a national standard for bright-light exposure.

Xerox participates in the activities of both National and International Standards groups and the National Safety Council both representation and information exchange. In addition, we offer full support to such endeavors as the annual United Way Fund-Raising Campaign. Included are Corporate donations, employee fund-raising, payroll deduction, and executives loaned to provide administrative support.

Xerox has a policy of ethical conduct to be maintained by its employees in relationships with customers, suppliers, government officials, candidates for political office, and political parties. In addition, there are ethical conduct policies tailored to specific situations: for employee purchase and sale of Xerox securities; to avoid conflicts of interest with outside business activities; for Materials Management personnel who deal with suppliers; for Finance personnel, who have unique stewardship responsibilities; and for Xerox people engaged in obtaining information about competitors to be used in benchmarking activities.

Each year the Chief Executive Office issues a letter to all company officers, directors, and key managers, reinterating our policy of ethical conduct and reminding everyone of his or her responsibility to understand and comply with the policy. Further, the recipients must confirm, in writing, the existence of a process for making employees aware of the policy. Xerox remains firmly committed to its responsibilities as a concerned and involved Corporate citizen.

2.0 Information and Analysis

Comprehensive data systems and analysis are the foundations for continuous quality improvement at Xerox.

- Xerox has over 375 major information systems supporting the total business. Over 175 of these systems relate specifically to the management, evaluation, and planning of quality.

- The validity, accuracy, and timeliness of the data management system are assured by Xerox' use of the Data Systems Quality Assurance process during the design, construction, and major upgrade of each data system.

- Xerox users require that data be easily accessible where and when it is needed. Xerox has one of the most extensive computer networks in the world, linking hundreds of Xerox sites on four continents to provide information twenty-four hours a day, seven days a week.

- The Quality Improvement Process (QIP) and Problem Solving Process (PSP) are used by teams across the entire company for quality improvement. The QIP is used as the structure for planning, organizing, and monitoring quality improvement efforts. The PSP is used for the determination of root causes of problems, development of countermeasures, and verification of the countermeasures' effectiveness.

- In order to assist teams in using the QIP and PSP, a software system available on all 30,000 Xerox workstations provides easy access to quality-related tools, including graphics and an "electronic facilitator" tool.

- QITs have been empowered to improve information-handling and tracking by applying the quality process to their daily problems.

- Xerox strives to improve the ways it collects and uses information to effect quality results. Recent examples include the development of Technology Readiness, which is a framework for bringing together all of the data needed to select technology for new products, and the Automated Installation Quality Report (AIQR) system. The AIQR system collects data on machines and customer sites; the data can then be used for more efficient service and product planning.

3.0 Planning for Quality

Planning translates customer requirements into benchmark products and services.

- Over a five-year period (1983 to 1988), Leadership Through Quality stimulated an evolution in the planning process: from an orientation toward financial performance to an orientation focused on satisfying customer requirements. Xerox believes that if it delivers world-class products and services that fully meet customer requirements, it will also reach its business goals.

- At Xerox, Leadership Through Quality provides the planning platform for developing both short- and long-term improvements: customer orientation, employee involvement, benchmarking, and use of quality tools.

- Xerox uses information-gathering systems, including market research studies (more than 180 studies in 1988 alone). Xerox uses the Business Resource Management System to allocate resources for specific projects consistent with customer requirements. Project teams have goals and targets based on customer requirements. Xerox knows that what its customers value most is copy quality, reliability, productivity, and operability.

- Xerox quality planning is fully integrated with formal business planning activities.

- Short- and long-term planning documents set measurable targets for both product quality and customer service, and indicate how the company's resources are deployed to meet customer requirements.

- At every stage, new-product plans and performance are checked not only against customer requirements and short-term targets, but against the performance of competitors' products and services. This is benchmarking, defined as "the continuous process of measuring our products, services, and practices against our toughest competitors, or those recognized as world leaders." Benchmarking can lead to changes in a product's design or scheduling. One example: Prior to launch in 1985, the 1065's projected performance was not at benchmark levels. Additional funding was allocated to improve the quality—which at launch was fifty-five percent better than benchmark.

The amount of benchmarking Xerox does has increased dramatically since 1984: from fourteen performance elements benchmarked to 237 elements today. Xerox measures itself against the industry average (the mean performance of companies in its industry), against the competitive benchmark (the best performance in its industry), and against the world-class benchmark (the best performance in any industry).

4.0 Human Resources

Within Team Xerox, quality improvement is the job of every employee.

- Xerox managers are directly accountable for the development and implementation of human resource plans, which are based on the quality requirements of the business.

- Embedded in Leadership Through Quality are six basic human resource improvement strategies: employee involvement, empowerment, training and development, management behavior change, recognition, and communications.

- All operating units have a senior personnel manager and a quality manager on their staffs to assist with planning. Unit plans are reviewed by the Corporate Personnel Council for consistency and effectiveness.

- Teams exist in every facet of Xerox; they are functional and cross-functional; involve union members, managers, suppliers, and customers; and may be multilocational or multinational in makeup.

- Joint union/management study teams to decide on cost-effective actions to retain work in-house were a provision of the 1983 union contract—a provision unique to American industry at that time.

- Teamwork Day participation has grown tenfold since the first event in 1983 and has been expanded to include customer and supplier participation.

- Every Xerox employee receives at least twenty-eight hours of quality training. Over the last four years, Xerox has invested more than four million employee hours and $125 million in quality training. All employees are trained in the core tools of quality; additional training is provided as necessary. Periodic surveys are conducted to identify new training needs as they arise. Training is uniform—common tools and processes are taught across all of Xerox, to all employees, creating a "common language" within Xerox to foster cohesive team functioning. After initial training, managers act as quality inspectors with their family groups, facilitating application of the tools learned. Quality specialists assist with this. Quality training is also reinforced in on-the-job use.

- Communication between employees and managers flows both ways. Input is sought from employees through the Employee Satisfaction Measurement System, the "COMMENT" program, and suggestion programs. Employee attitude survey responses to the statement, "Sufficient effort is made to get the opinions and thinking of people who work here," have remained above the industry norms for the past four years. Manager walk-arounds, the "Open Door" policy, surveys, round tables, communications meetings, and executive interviews (conducted with one's manager's manager) further increase employee-manager communication.

- Results from Xerox Employee Attitude Survey (XEAS), Employee Satisfaction and Motivation Survey (ESMS), special event follow-up surveys, and communication vehicles such as round tables, become the basis for action and employee feedback in a closed-loop process.

- Xerox has generously shared its approach to quality, including training, with many other companies including: General Motors, Ford Motor Company, Corning Glass, Motorola, Florida Power and Light, American Standard, Proctor and Gamble, and numerous government agencies and unions.

- Recognition is another key aspect of Leadership Through Quality. Current recognition programs strike a balance between honoring individual effort and teamwork. Team-oriented awards include the Team Excellence Award and Excellence in Customer Satisfaction. Individual recognition vehicles include the President's Award and the Xerox Achievement Award. Over forty percent of all recognition vehicles can be initiated by peer nomination. In addition to awards, Xerox employees share in Xerox achievement through gain sharing, profit sharing, and various financial incentive programs.

- Xerox safeguards the health and safety of its employees and customers. The Office of Environmental Health and Safety (OSHA) coordinates all aspects of health and safety, including fire protection, toxicology, product safety, environmental issues, and occupational medicine. Throughout Xerox, from product design to work practices, the emphasis is on eliminating the root causes of safety problems. Standards are set and monitored by various safety committees; safety performance is audited periodically. All this attention to safety has paid off: Xerox has never had either an industrial fatality or a major OSHA citation.

- Employee job security is addressed at Xerox in various ways: through retraining as needed, through opportunities for Voluntary Reduction In Force and early retirement, and through redeployment. Personal security is also a consideration: Xerox provides its employees with Xerox Family Security Plans, Retirement Income Guarantee Plans, confidential family and personal assistance when they are needed, and access to recreation and health management programs.

- Other key employee measurements are attendance, turnover, ratings of work climate, and days lost to occupational injury or illness. Each of these has shown improvement in the last few years. Xerox attendance is above the industrial average. Turnover has shown a dramatic thirty-six percent improvement since 1985.

5.0 Quality Assurance

Xerox quality processes assure quality Xerox products.

- Product and service quality is assured through the Xerox Delivery Process. It combines the Product Delivery Process, which is centered on product development and manufacturing, and the Customer Delivery Process, which is centered on the operating units responsible for sales and field customer support.

- Product Development Teams are headed by a chief engineer and own the goals of the program from concept to beyond product launch.

- Several aspects of the Xerox Delivery Process contribute to its effectiveness: Phase Gate Reviews, built in at many points, which not only evaluate progress, but anticipate future project needs; attention at each step to customer requirements; repeated and varied testing at each stage of product development to evaluate performance; and consistent emphasis on preventing problems. The Xerox Delivery Process is monitored by two committees: the Product Delivery Process Cabinet, a steering committee of line managers in product development, and the Customer Satisfaction Improvement Committee. QITs investigate and correct any process problems.

- The Product Delivery Team includes people from product planning, design engineering, product safety, human factors, field logistics, service, marketing support, sales operations, and the Manufacturing Resource Team, a cross-functional team within manufacturing.

- Product development testing takes the perspective of the customer. Internal measures of product quality by the Product Delivery Team are related to external measures by the Customer Satisfaction Measurement System. In addition, both Field Readiness Demonstration Tests and Customer Acceptance Tests are customer-centered assessments designed to detect potential issues in the ability to deliver products prior to the launch date.

- Xerox suppliers are eligible to participate in the Xerox training program, which includes instruction on cycle time, quality, statistics, and product design as well as visits to benchmark suppliers to see these techniques in practice. This is one illustration of the partnership between Xerox and its suppliers.

6.0 Quality Results

Xerox products and services are industry benchmarks.

- Xerox customers' major product quality requirements are copy quality, reliability, operability, and productivity. Over the past six years, Xerox has shown quality improvements in each of these areas.

- In order to assess Xerox quality results against those of our competitors, Xerox tests its equipment in its Competitive Products Laboratory. It also uses outside rating agencies. These sources confirm that Xerox has led its industry in copy quality every year since 1985. Some Xerox printers offer resolution that is twice that of the best competing units. Xerox also leads the field in toner performance and paper performance.

- Xerox quality improvement activities have yielded ever-increasing internal operating efficiencies. Use of Cost of Quality tools and processes, in particular, have resulted in lowered manufacturing costs, overhead rates, inventory levels, and lead times for the production of new goods. Many of these improvements have been brought about by QITs using Leadership Through Quality processes.

- Product quality improved from a 1980 base by over ninety percent despite an increasingly severe measurement criteria for total defect reporting, and was at benchmark performance level by 1988.

- Unscheduled maintenance improved forty percent from 1984 to 1988.

- Machine availability doubled from 1984 to 1988.

- Copy quality of new machines improved fifty percent from 1984 to 1988 and clearly exceeded Xerox' best competitors' products by 1985.

- Service response time improved twenty-seven percent from 1984 to 1988.

- Suppliers' quality improved sixty percent from 1986 to 1988 and is clearly the industry benchmark.

- The number of parts requiring an inspection at receiving was reduced by ninety-three percent from 1981 to 1988.

7.0 Customer Satisfaction

Customer Satisfaction is the number one Xerox priority.

- Six strategies integrate data about customers with management action. These are: customer obsession, a focus on making customer satisfaction the number one priority; the District Partnerships, created to increase cross-functional focus on common goals related to customer satisfaction; an information technology strategy, to bring quality-related information to the District Partnerships; business simplification, to make it easier for customers to do business with Xerox; customer-focus marketing, to address the differing needs of various market segments; and empowerment, to bring to bear all the talents and expertise of every Xerox employee.

- Xerox uses a wide variety of methods to gather information about customers: market research studies, customer satisfaction surveys, external industry surveys, third-party competitive benchmarking surveys, XPLOR users group, Executive Communication Exchange Center forums, customer focus groups, and direct customer contact by the sales, service, telemarketing, and administrative personnel.

- Xerox also makes it easy for customers to voice their requirements via toll-free numbers, hot lines, extensive follow-ups, and customer-contact employees who have received additional empowerments to resolve customer issues. Examples of such empowerments include self-managing service work groups and sale reversal authority at the District level. Customer-contact employees are supported by extensive technology, including automated systems that can provide nearly any piece of information required about a product, a process, or even an individual machine.

- Standards have been set and exceeded for customer service.

Executives have responsibility for "focus accounts" and for customer complaint response. Customers rated Xerox ninety-nine percent for professionalism of service personnel. Customer satisfaction with Sales telephone follow-up is also ninety-nine percent. Telephone waiting time has shown a three-year improvement of twenty-eight percent and is now sixteen percent better than industry standard. Refunds for sales reversals have dropped twenty-nine percent, while billing transaction quality improved thirty-five percent. Again, the major means for achieving these successes has been Leadership Through Quality processes.

- For the past eight years, Xerox' major method for assessing customer satisfaction has been CSMS. Each month 55,000 surveys are mailed to customers, asking them to rate Xerox equipment, sales, service, and customer administration performance. Complaints are reviewed monthly at all levels to identify root causes and devise solutions. Since 1984, the number of complaints received by the Office of the President has dropped by sixty percent.

The resulting data is segmented into nine categories and given comprehensive analysis. The next step is to translate analysis into quality improvements. Short-term concerns are referred to the District for resolution. Monthly reviews at the District, regional, and national levels focus on strategies for improvement. Annual comprehensive reviews set the next year's customer satisfaction targets by product category; these are then incorporated into the organizations' operating plans.

- During 1987 and 1988, the percentage of highly satisfied customers increased from sixty-seven percent to seventy-two percent.

- Xerox has a three-year warranty and a "no questions asked" return policy that outdistances its competitors.

- Following a six-percent market share loss from 1984 to 1985 to Japanese competitors, Xerox regained 2.8 percent share by 1988.

- Xerox customer retention averages 90.5 percent against an industry average of seventy-five percent.

Board of Examiners Feedback Report

Each applicant for the Malcolm Baldrige National Quality Award receives a feedback report from the Board of Examiners. The feedback report summarizes the findings and observations of the examiners. It reports both strengths and areas for improvement by each of the examination categories. The 1989 Xerox feedback report from the Board of Examiners is summarized in the following sections. The wording has been preserved, except for slight changes to improve textual clarity.

Scoring Summary

The determination of a site visit is based upon the score of each applicant relative to the other applicants in their class. Xerox applied as a large manufacturing business. In 1989, forty applicants received a first-stage review of their written applications, twenty-three were assessed at the second-stage consensus review, and ten companies received a site visit. Of those ten companies, eight were manufacturing companies and two were in the service category.

The Board of Examiners does not disclose the exact score of a company's application, but it does report the range of the score. Xerox Business Products and Systems scored in the range of 751 to 875 of the total 1000 points. Xerox provided evidence of effective performance in all seven categories and an outstanding performance in Category 6.0 - Quality Results and Category 7.0 - Customer Satisfaction. The Board of Examiners Feedback Report stated:

"Xerox has an excellent quality-oriented management team whose efforts are reflected through enthusiastic employee involvement in Quality Improvement Teams (QITs), uniform understanding of quality policy and mission statements, intensive training programs, and the use of manufacturing and service industry benchmarks to measure customer satisfaction. The overall scoring results reflect the achievement of the Leadership Through Quality concept, which began in 1983, to regain and increase market share. The Xerox approach emphasizes customer satisfaction through quality improvements."

In addition to the overall comments, the Board of Examiners also identifies areas of strength and improvement for each of the seven categories of the award criteria. The following paragraphs provide the examiners' detailed observations of the Xerox strengths and areas for improvement.

1.0 Leadership

Strengths

- Xerox Business Products and Systems demonstrates a very high and visible level of leadership interest in the quality management practices and improvement processes.

- Managers at all levels, including the Chairman/Chief Executive Officer and President, are personally involved in the quality planning process and in communicating quality improvement objectives. They are also active in supporting external quality-related activities.

- Quality values are communicated to all employees in the Green Book, Xerox World, and in training and reference material.

- Management has granted each employee the authority to stop a line or process because of quality problems.

- Management recognizes outstanding Quality Improvement Team (QIT) projects by setting aside a special Teamwork Day each year to showcase quality improvements. All employees are encouraged to attend.

Areas for Improvement

- It appears that suppliers' accessibility to senior executives is limited and not fully deployed on a routine basis.

2.0 Information and Analysis

Strengths

- The scope and availability of data is excellent with 375 information systems, of which 175 are specifically related to the management, evaluation, and planning of quality.

- Analyses of data are performed for a prevention-based approach to identify quality improvements.

- Quality improvement analytical and statistical tools are used effectively for prevention and quality improvement purposes.

- An average end-to-end response time of 2.5 seconds is better than the industry average.

Areas for Improvement

- The key quality systems have been in place for less than two years, and their full effectiveness and use have not been realized.

3.0 Strategic Quality Planning

Strengths

- Strategic quality planning is integrated into the total business planning process.

- Customer satisfaction is the foundation of the Xerox planning process.

- The planning process makes extensive use of benchmarking by using a long-term approach without trade-offs for short-term profits.

Areas for Improvement

- Strategic quality planning appears to be less effective and not fully deployed in manufacturing areas.

- The quality planning process is relatively new and not fully matured as a system.

4.0 Human Resource Utilization

Strengths

- Utilization of the work force potential has been enhanced through extensive training, attitude surveys, and empowerment to act.

- Both attitude and customer surveys are used to establish individual objectives at all levels of management and business segments.

- The site visit revealed a spirit of informality, openness, cooperation, and loyalty among employees that is supportive of the company's quality goals.

- Excellent quality of work life factors are provided to employees and have been recognized by external accolades.

- There is a high degree of employee involvement in Quality Improvement Teams, and employees readily acknowledge management's support for their efforts.

Areas for Improvement

- As evidenced by attitude survey results, the transition from a reactive system to a proactive system is not fully implemented.

- Training records reflect attendance but lack a measure of the skills acquired and implemented.

5.0 Quality Assurance of Products and Services

Strengths

- An excellent "seamless delivery" process, which has been refined over twenty years, ensures the delivery of reliable products in a timely manner. It consists of both a Product Delivery Process and a Customer Delivery Process.

- The Commodity Management process has been very successful in improving the quality of supplied materials and parts.

- Excellent training and recognition programs are provided for suppliers.

- Applications of Statistical Process Control are understood, and process capabilities are determined for each process applicable to new products.

- An excellent documentation system, which covers major functions, processes, and benchmarking data, has been provided.

- Internal operating standards are established based upon information obtained from customers, employees, benchmarks, and corporate objectives.

- Excellent applications of Quality Improvement Teams and Continuous Supplier Involvement programs are used to achieve Process Qualification for direct shipments.

- Audit activities are utilized effectively to improve operating systems, identify potential improvements, reduce the number of defects, and aid in management's actions.

Areas for Improvement

- There is a lack of evidence of the effectiveness of the Customer Services Engineer Planning Model.

- Evidence that was evaluated reflects an emphasis on prevention. However, in some inspection areas where control charts are used to determine corrective action, no evidence is given that preventive measures are implemented.

6.0 Quality Results

Strengths

- There is a strong motivation toward satisfaction and an excellent response to adverse customer reactions.

- Quality results have been a positive influence in a competitive environment, resulting in an increase of market share.

- An excellent benchmarking program is utilized which focuses on "the best" anywhere in the world.

- Significant improvements have been achieved by the reduction of suppliers and the implementation of a supplier certification program.

- Parts inventory has been significantly reduced through the use of an aggressive Just-In-Time program

Areas for Improvement

- The sources of data were not always clearly identified.

7.0 Customer Satisfaction

Strengths

- Excellent systems are in place to determine customer satisfaction.

- Liability claims have been significantly reduced during the last five years.

- Each day a different officer of the corporation is assigned to handle those customer complaints that cannot be resolved at a lower level.

- A significant drop in customer complaints has occurred during the past five years.

- An automatic service scheduling system, which is presently being tested, will detect problems in the customer's equipment before they occur.

- The Customer Satisfaction Measurement System indicates that the number of products returned has been reduced approximately one-half over the last five years.

- Customer complaints are addressed immediately. Xerox has a goal of resolving ninety-five percent of the complaints in less than two days and 100 percent within five days.

Areas for Improvement

- Although there is a high level of satisfied customers, Xerox products were ranked second in low-, medium-, and high-volume products.

The Value of the application process

Winning the Malcolm Baldrige National Quality Award was a great honor for Xerox. However, the greatest value came from the application process where potential company improvements were identified. Xerox exited the NQA challenge with a clearer vision of the changes necessary to maintain its competitive position and pursue ever-improving business excellence.

Chapter Five
Calibrating the Business

The Baldrige Award application was prepared over a relatively short period, but the lessons learned by Team Xerox have been enduring. As the NQA Team members began to write their responses to the forty-four examination items of the Baldrige Award criteria, they noticed gaps between what they wanted to say about Xerox quality and what could be supported by facts. They observed broken processes that did not produce the desired output. They found that some necessary data was not available. They also found that some of the data being collected was not usable. The team did not have the capability to improve the quality system as it developed the application so they decided to record all of the improvement opportunities they observed in order to address them appropriately after the application and site visit were completed.

Life after Baldrige

After the team members completed the Baldrige Award application, they analyzed this list of quality opportunities, or "warts." The team compared current state and desired state for each opportunity to access the magnitude of the gap and to identify causal relationships and root causes as well as target areas for improvement. At first, this task seemed overwhelming, but then the team used the quality tools to sort through the mass number of improvements needed and identify those critical few areas needing immediate attention. They categorized the list into two fundamental principles and eleven areas for improvement (described in the following paragraph). The team used quality methods and tools to complete the analysis. This was a bottoms-up analysis used to discover the vital few areas that required priority improvement in each business area. Members grouped the opportunities into separate clusters using an affinity diagraming technique. They assembled data for each cluster and formed problem statements to determine gaps for each area of concern. Finally, they created large cause-and-effect analysis diagrams to recommend countermeasures to the identified root causes of the areas for improvement.

The analysis process resulted in a total of fifty-one specific actions, which were recommended to senior management in December 1989. Even though the company was celebrating the receipt of the Baldrige Award, Xerox was still moving forward to improve itself. Although the results from the Baldrige assessment showed that Xerox was good by an external standard, Xerox was not satisfied because all of the gaps between the current state and the desired state were not closed. In this spirit of continuous improvement and with the commitment to continue the journey, Xerox management wanted to stretch the entire organization toward the theoretical limits of excellence in both customer satisfaction and productivity.

Correcting problems means understanding the gaps

The two fundamental principles identified in the assessment were the need for increased emphasis on both "management by fact" and continuous improvement. The assessment team grouped the fifty-one recommended actions into eleven categories. Management by fact and continuous improvement shortfalls were common gaps in all eleven categories. The assessment team concluded that all levels of the corporation needed a change in mind-set in order to make progress in these two critical dimensions of quality.

"Management by fact" was used within Xerox to mean the collection and analysis of data for a given issue before making plans and decisions, rather than relying on intuition, past practice, or opinion. Continuous improvement meant that Xerox would constantly develop its people, improve its work processes, and upgrade those things in the environment necessary to produce the work desired by its customers.

These two principles were derived from the calibration process that the assessment team used to identify problem areas compared to the questions raised by the Baldrige Award criteria. In addition, Xerox had gained stunning insights that would influence its way of thinking about the approach to quality and improving its deployment at Xerox. The following insights summarize the eleven categories for focused, continuous, world-wide improvement on the solid base established by the pre-Baldrige efforts and were to be addressed over the next five years:

1. Total customer satisfaction: Customer satisfaction, as the number one business priority, must consistently drive management discussions, decisions, actions, planning, spending, and operational business processes.

2. Total employee satisfaction: The creative and emotional involvement of all employees must be captured to improve employee satisfaction to industry average. Employee involvement must continue to improve in order to achieve a leadership position in customer satisfaction, because the behavior and morale of employees is a leading indicator that gauges how customers will feel about Xerox products and services in the future. Employee satisfaction was elevated to become the fourth corporate-wide priority in 1991.

3. Management role model behavior: A consistent set of role model management standards must be used as the basis for selecting people for promotion. Effective coaching processes should be provided to help managers mature in their skill to apply quality processes.

4. Market-in orientation: Managers must more effectively use customer expectations to make decisions and establish objectives rather than relying on their judgment and personal experience.

5. Process excellence: Xerox must continue its efforts to document, standardize, and continuously improve its work processes which produce business results.

6. Error reduction: Xerox must increase the use of measurements for work process outputs and record the actual number of errors that are produced in order to accumulate the data necessary to identify and eliminate the root causes of problems.

7. Policy deployment: Xerox must consistently deploy processes that allow all employees, as individuals, to show how their work contributes to the company's objectives. This process will allow the organization to confirm the alignment of its effort to meet overall business objectives.

8. Product and customer service goals: Xerox must establish breakthrough goals for continuous improvement of all key competitive competencies that support its products and services based on the requirements of its customers.

9. Benchmarking: Benchmarking must be extended as a practice across all levels and within all functions of the organization.

10. Quality training and application: Xerox must further develop the ability of all employees to use quality tools to help improve business results.

11. Physical work environment: Xerox must enhance the work environment necessary to satisfy employees and contribute to employee productivity.

Management reviewed these recommendations and the findings from operations reviews and planning sessions held for fiscal year 1990. Based on that information, they established the following six planks as the basis for the intensification of Leadership Through Quality activities during the 1990s:

- Ensure that customers continue to define Xerox business.

- Management should more aggressively develop, articulate, and deploy clear direction and objectives.

- Work process improvements as the means to meet operational goals.

- Maintain the quality role of the line management: "Quality in the line - by the line."

- Take productive steps to improve employee motivation and empowerment.

- Increase training, communications, and quality support.

These planks became the focal point for the senior management team as they defined a sub-set of twenty-five actions related to the intensification of Leadership Through Quality over the five-year period from 1991 to 1995. The process of sorting through and evaluating the lessons of the quality pursuit was tedious. It had also resulted in a cornucopia of outputs: fifty-one actions, eleven categories, two principles, six planks, and a sub-set of twenty-five actions. Xerox recognized the need for a more unified structure to serve as the basis for its Quality Intensification.

Intensifying the commitment to Leadership Through Quality

In early January 1990, senior management divided the sub-set of twenty-five actions into those which would be key priorities for implementation in 1990. A senior manager was assigned to track and manage progress of these priorities. The first principle the team reviewed was "Reinforce the use of work process improvements as the means to meet operational goals."

During 1990, this action was "first among equals" in terms of management's attention and effort in improving quality at Xerox. In an effort to support the internal Xerox capabilities in work process improvement, the company worked with Fuji Xerox to arrange for the coaching of senior management by two members of JUSE. Dr. Hajime Makabe and Dr. Noriaki Kano continue to help coach members of the senior management team in the area of work process improvement. Later, Xerox hired Boston Consulting Group to help identify high priority actions to meet its work process improvement for product time-to-market operational goal.

Defining quality in business operations

By the middle of 1991, the Quality Intensification effort was receiving a great deal of management attention. Some of the senior executives observed that the quality agenda, although founded upon sound management principles, looked more like an unorganized "laundry list" rather than a well structured, focused quality strategy. One member of the Allaire team suggested that Xerox needed an operational definition of Leadership Through Quality. It was also suggested that a Leadership Through Quality annual assessment should be integrated into the annual planning process to encourage continuous improvement. The idea behind this suggestion was to link the cycle of quality diagnosis with the resource-allocating process found within the annual operational planning process. This tight coupling of policy deployment for work process improvement activities with current business issues facilitated a diagnostic review in the annual quality self-assessment to identify the root causes of business problems or opportunities which, in turn, guided the assignment of resources to implement countermeasures as work process improvements. This assessment system would be a structured system developed upon the foundation of the analysis from the Quality Intensification effort.

Xerox created an assessment system for Leadership Through Quality and positioned it as part of the management process that would be used in the development of the operating plan for each unit. The following five principles guided this renewed intensification of Leadership Through Quality:

- Fully satisfy customer-defined requirements.

- Top management would lead by example.

- Involve, empower, and satisfy employees.

- Improve results in continuous process improvements by reducing:
  - Variability in work process performance
  - Cycle time through process improvement
  - Costs by reducing both variability and cycle time

- Integrate continuous quality improvement into the daily management of the business.

Operational Definition

So, to bring structure to all of this learning, Xerox moved back to the basics of assessing current state performance, identifying desired state performance and the gap between these two. Focusing on the critical few actions to close the gap.

This company-wide quality assessment approach was developed and deployed in early 1991, based on the lessons learned since the beginning of the Xerox quality experience. The inputs for the definition were the quality principles and models found in the Green Book, the Baldrige Award criteria, the European Quality Award criteria, and the lessons learned from the Xerox quality intensification assessment (see Figure 5.1). This operational definition of Leadership Through Quality consists of an assessment model that has six categories: management leadership, human resource management, process management, customer focus, quality support and tools, and results. The customer is at the center of this model. The objective of the model is to focus on the customer using the four enablers of management leadership, human resource management, process management, and quality support and tools to drive business results.

Each of the six categories of this Leadership Through Quality operational definition has a desired state, which is defined in terms of the vision of Xerox as a world-class company (see Figure 5.2). The forty elements that support

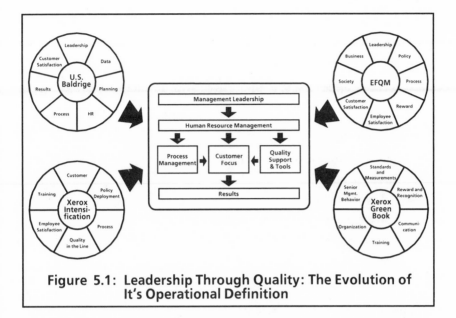

Figure 5.1: Leadership Through Quality: The Evolution of It's Operational Definition

this vision are mapped into the six categories (this system is informally called the "six by forty" assessment). Each of these elements has an identified measure that is used to assess progress.

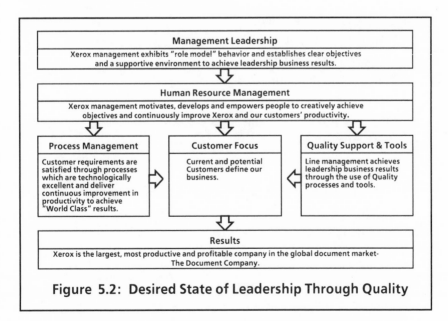

Figure 5.2: Desired State of Leadership Through Quality

The operational definition of Leadership Through Quality

The six major categories in the Leadership Through Quality assessment, along with their desired state and supporting elements, are:

- **Management Leadership**
  Desired State: Management exhibits "role model" behavior and establishes clear objectives and a supportive environment to achieve leadership business results.

  Supporting elements include:
  — Quality values and leadership
  — Strategic planning
  — Policy deployment
  — Management by fact
  — Employee communication
  — People empowerment
  — External responsibility

- **Human Resource Management**
  Desired State: Management motivates, develops, and empowers people to creatively achieve objectives and continuously improve Xerox and Xerox customers' productivity.

  Supporting elements include:
  — Selection and recruitment
  — Education and training
  — Management development
  — Reward and recognition
  — Employee involvement and suggestions
  — Work environment

- **Process Management**
  Desired State: Customer requirements are satisfied through processes that are technologically superior, and deliver continuous improvement in productivity to achieve "world-class" results.

  Supporting elements include:
  — Business process management
  — Continuous improvement
  — Process control measures
  — Information utilization
  — Better practices

— Technological superiority
— Quality, cost, and delivery (QCD)
— Supplier quality, cost, and delivery (QCD)

- **Customer Focus**
Desired State: Current and potential customers define the business.

Supporting elements include:
— "Customer First"
— Customer database
— Market segments
— Customer requirements
— Customer satisfaction measurement system
— Customer query and complaint management
— Customer gains and losses
— Customer relationship management
— Customer commitment
— Customer communications

- **Quality Support and Tools**
Desired State: Line management achieves leadership business results through the use of quality processes and tools.

Supporting elements include:
— Benchmarking
— Problem Solving Process, Quality Improvement Process
— Statistical and advanced tools
— Quality Network
— Unit-unique tools as defined by the line management team

- **Results**
Desired State: Xerox is the largest, most productive and profitable company in the global document market—The Document Company.

Supporting elements include:
— Customer satisfaction performance
— Employee motivation and satisfaction performance
— Market share performance
— Return on assets performance

Measuring quality improvement

This working definition of Leadership Through Quality became the integral assessment guideline for the measurement of quality improvement from one planning cycle to another. Each of the forty elements is evaluated on a seven-point scale as shown in Figure 5.3. The gap between the current state

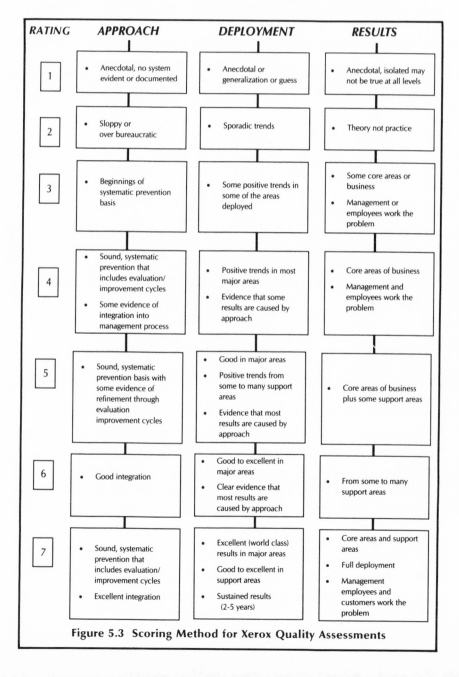

RATING	APPROACH	DEPLOYMENT	RESULTS
1	• Anecdotal, no system evident or documented	• Anecdotal or generalization or guess	• Anecdotal, isolated may not be true at all levels
2	• Sloppy or over bureaucratic	• Sporadic trends	• Theory not practice
3	• Beginnings of systematic prevention basis	• Some positive trends in some of the areas deployed	• Some core areas or business • Management or employees work the problem
4	• Sound, systematic prevention that includes evaluation/ improvement cycles • Some evidence of integration into management process	• Positive trends in most major areas • Evidence that some results are caused by approach	• Core areas of business • Management and employees work the problem
5	• Sound, systematic prevention basis with some evidence of refinement through evaluation improvement cycles	• Good in major areas • Positive trends from some to many support areas • Evidence that most results are caused by approach	• Core areas of business plus some support areas
6	• Good integration	• Good to excellent in major areas • Clear evidence that most results are caused by approach	• From some to many support areas
7	• Sound, systematic prevention that includes evaluation/ improvement cycles • Excellent integration	• Excellent (world class) results in major areas • Good to excellent in support areas • Sustained results (2-5 years)	• Core areas and support areas • Full deployment • Management employees and customers work the problem

Figure 5.3 Scoring Method for Xerox Quality Assessments

and the desired state for each of the forty elements is used to identify where effort should be placed for improvement during the next planning cycle. Specific emphasis in the operating plan is placed on the vital few elements identified during this assessment. Year-to-year progress is tracked by using the same assessment mechanism and comparing progress achieved over the prior assessments. Figure 5.4 illustrates the assessment scheme as it developed from the initial application of Leadership Through Quality through the Baldrige Award assessment to the self-assessments administered by each of the business divisions.

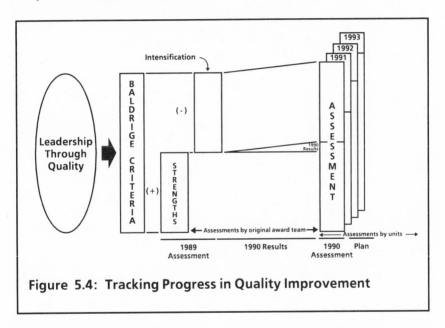

Figure 5.4: Tracking Progress in Quality Improvement

Managing for results

Xerox learned that the closed-loop planning process is essential to assuring that identified improvement goals are actually achieved. Figure 5.5 shows in more detail how the assessment tool is used to measure progress. In-process measures for each of the forty elements are correlated with business results. The diagnosis of problems in the area of business results indicates which of the forty elements needs attention to improve performance in the following planning cycle. These key elements are identified as the vital few for attention while the operating plan of the assessed entity for the next year is developed. The policy deployment process provides the linkage between the initial diagnosis of the problems, the setting of organizational objectives, and the deployment of them to the employee level. This process was called

"Managing For Results" in the United States and "Policy Deployment" in both Rank Xerox and Fuji Xerox. Figure 5.6 illustrates the major steps in this deployment process and the linkage from the corporate direction to the annual objectives of individuals. The new contribution of this process to the Leadership Through Quality operational definition was that it established linkage between the measurement of process performance, diagnosis of

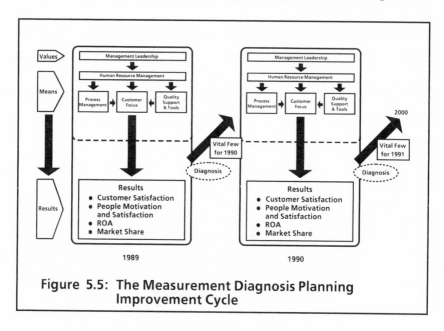

Figure 5.5: The Measurement Diagnosis Planning Improvement Cycle

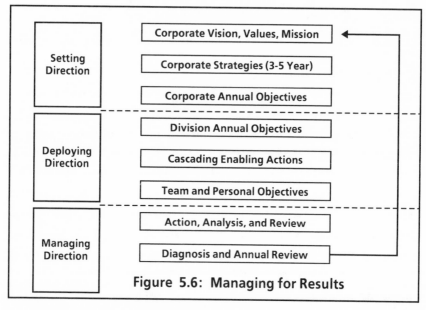

Figure 5.6: Managing for Results

problem areas, and definition of responsibility for action to improve the process. Congruence in these steps of the planning process assures improved alignment between the strategic direction of the corporation and the actions of Xerox teams and individual employees as well as focuses the corporation's limited resources on the vital few strategic actions.

Implementing the Methodology

In 1990, the United States Marketing Group (USMG) component of the Xerox Business Products and Systems organization decided to implement this assessment process throughout its 32,000 employee organization. The approach used was to certify each operating entity within USMG using the assessment criteria to validate its quality improvements. To be certified, an operating unit had to achieve a minimum of 400 points using the Baldrige Award criteria. Over 140 operating entities were assessed by a team of fifty internal examiners from April 1990 through June 1991. These internal examiners were members of the USMG Senior Staff and the Corporate Quality Office. Thus, this new team became more knowledgeable and committed to TQM. Six units achieved world-class distinction (above 751 points on the Baldrige scoring system) while five units did not initially qualify. Eventually, all units passed at the minimum level. Today, this baseline serves as a standard for assessing those critical few areas that need improvement within an operating unit and for measuring improvement over time.

Rank Xerox also adapted this assessment methodology in a similar way for its Business Excellence Certification, which is highlighted in their application for the European Quality Award.

Organizational Assessment and Reflection

Thus, the intensive learning of the post-Baldrige analysis was finally distilled into a logically cohesive process for assessment and improvement which yields continuous improvement in a defined set of vital few areas, year after year in every Xerox entity - each aligned to defined corporate goals and objectives.

Chapter Six
Making Mid-course Corrections

The European Quality Award is sponsored jointly by three organizations: The European Commission (EC), The European Foundation for Quality Management (EFQM), and The European Organization for Quality (EOQ). The European Commission is the governing coordinating body for thirteen European nations. The EFQM, formed by nearly 200 leading European businesses in 1988, is committed to promoting quality as the fundamental process for continuous improvement within a business. The European Organization for Quality (EOQ) is a federation of twenty-five national quality associations. It was established in 1957 with the aim of improving quality and reliability of products and services. These three organizations jointly created the European Quality Award to enhance the position of Western European businesses by:

- Accelerating the acceptance of quality as a strategy for global competitive advantage

- Stimulating and assisting the deployment of quality improvement activities

The European Quality Award offers two levels of recognition to applicants. The first is the European Quality Prize, which is awarded to companies that demonstrate excellence in the management of quality as their process for continuous improvement. The second level is the European Quality Award, which is awarded to the most successful advocate of Total Quality Management (TQM) in Western Europe. The European Quality Prize and the European Quality Award were granted for the first time in 1992.

Successful applicants must demonstrate that their approach to TQM has contributed significantly over the past few years to satisfying the expectations of customers, employees, and others with an interest in the company. A prize-winning company is one that has excelled in the European marketplace. All applicants must have a significant business commitment to Western Europe. At least fifty percent of the applicant's operations must have been conducted within Western Europe during the past five years. The quality practices on which the application is based are subject to inspection in Western Europe; all of the applicants' sites must be open to inspection by teams of EQA examiners.

Award criteria

The award criteria are based upon a model for Total Quality Management developed jointly by the European Commission, the European Foundation for Quality Management and the European Organization for Quality. The core element of the application material is the self-appraisal of an organization's quality progress using this standard quality model for the sake of consistency. The model contains nine elements and serves as a criterion for self-assessment of an organization's journey toward implementing Total Quality Management. The first five elements of the model are labeled "enablers" which are concerned with the strategies, methods, and programs which define how results are achieved. The final four elements are labeled "results" which are concerned with what the organization has achieved in the past, its current performance, and improvement trends for key business measures and process factors. This model is encouraged for self-appraisal by organizations: the regular and systematic review of the organization's activities and results. The objective of a self-appraisal system is to rigorously review each of these nine criteria and, based on the findings, to adopt relevant improvement strategies. The following summary describes the European Quality Award criteria.

Enablers

1.0 Leadership
The behavior of all managers in driving the organization toward Total Quality.

- 1a. Involvement in leading quality management.
- 1b. Total Quality culture.
- 1c. Recognition and appreciation of the efforts and successes of individuals and teams.
- 1d. Support of Total Quality by provision of appropriate resources and assistance.
- 1e. Involvement with customers and suppliers.

1f. Active promotion of quality management outside the organization.

2.0 Policy and Strategy
The organization's values, vision, and strategic direction, and the ways in which the organization achieves them.

2a. How policy and strategy are based on the concept of Total Quality.

2b. How policy and strategy are determined using relevant information.

2c. How policy and strategy are the basis of business plans.

2d. How policy and strategy are communicated.

2e. How policy and strategy are regularly reviewed and improved.

3.0 People Management
The management of the organization's people.

3a. How continuous improvement in people management is effected.

3b. How the organization preserves and develops core skills through the recruitment, training, and career progression of its people.

3c. How the organization's performance targets are agreed and are reviewed continuously with staff.

3d. How the organization promotes the involvement of all its people in quality and continuous improvement.

4.0 Resources
The management, utilization, and preservation of resources.

4a. Financial resources.

4b. Information resources.

4c. Material resources.

4d. Application of technology.

5.0 Processes
The management of all the value-adding activities within the organization.

5a. How key processes are identified.

5b. How the organization systematically manages its key and support processes.

5c. How process performance parameters, along with all relevant feedback are used to review key processes and to set targets for improvement.

5d. How the organization stimulates innovation and creativity in process improvement.

5e. How the organization implements process changes and evaluates the benefits.

Results

6.0 Customer Satisfaction
What the perception of external customers, direct and indirect, is of the organization and of its products and services.

7.0 People Satisfaction
What the people's feelings are about their organization.

8.0 Impact on Society
What the perception of the organization is among society at large. This includes views of the organization's approach to quality of life, the environment, and to the preservation of global resources.

9.0 Business Results
What the organization is achieving in relation to its planned business performance.

For each enabler criteria the written application must provide the following required information:

- How the company approaches the criterion. Each criterion covers a range of specific areas as defined in the award brochure and concise and factual information should be provided to address these areas.

- The extent to which the approach has been deployed both vertically throughout all levels of the organization and horizontally across all business areas and activities.

- The key parameters used to measure results for each of the results categories.

- For each key parameter, data is required with trends presented to illustrate three years or more of history. The trends should highlight the following:

- The company's own targets.
- The relevance of parameters to all groups with an interest in the company (customers, employees, etc.)
- The company's actual performance (may be indexed for financial information), and where appropriate,
- The performance of competitors, and/or
- The performance of best in class organizations.

Application review process

The scoring of applications is divided into two 500-point segments, which are categorized as enablers (segments 1 through 5) and results (segments 6 through 9). The enablers are scored on the combination of two factors: the excellence of the approach and the degree of deployment of the approach. Results are scored based on a combination of two factors: the excellence and scope of the results.

The European Quality Award review process is modeled after the Baldrige process. Each 1992 application was assigned to a team of five to six assessors. It was first scored by each member of the team independently. The senior assessor then led a meeting in which the team presented its findings, debated the merits of the application against the award criteria, and arrived at a consensus score and assessment which reflected their findings. Their consensus score and findings were presented to a team of jurors. The jurors were appointed to oversee the assessment process and select applicants who were to receive either the award or one of the prizes. The jurors selected applicants that were to receive site visits based on the information provided in the consensus reports. Site visits were conducted to verify the statements in the application and clarify areas that were unclear. The site visit team had the authority to amend the original consensus score if appropriate. Following the site visit, the team would submit a final report to the jurors. On the basis of the site visit reports received, the jurors selected the applicants who would receive the award and the applicants who would receive a prize. All applicants received feedback reports which reflected the findings of the assessors in terms of strengths and areas for improvement based on the consensus report and, if conducted, the findings of the site visit.

For detailed information about the European Quality Award and the detailed self-assessment requirement, contact:

> The European Quality Award Secretariat
> European Foundation for Quality Management
> Avenue des Pleiades 19
> B-1200 Brussels
> Belgium
> Telephone: 322 7753511
> Telefax: 322 7791237

Rank Xerox application process

Late in 1991, Rank Xerox management decided to apply for the 1992 European Quality Award. This decision was based on a desire to intensify the ten-year effort of implementing Total Quality Management within all Rank Xerox operating units. Senior management viewed the external assessment of Rank Xerox by EQA officials as a common goal across all functional and national boundaries. It was felt that the application process would motivate employees and demonstrate management's commitment to continuous quality improvement.

The Rank Xerox strategy for applying for the award was to submit an application for the total Western European operations of Rank Xerox—fifteen country businesses, four manufacturing plants, a research center, and the international headquarters. The application would involve as many employees as possible in the development of an open and honest assessment of the company. This is common to all Xerox quality award applications. The assessment would evaluate the company's strength of commitment; diversity of approach across multiple cultures, languages, and nations; consistency of deployment; and the linkage to solid business results.

Based on lessons learned from the pursuit of the Baldrige award, a small core team was formed in January 1992 to gather information and write the application. Six people from different parts of the company were selected to represent a wide variety of skills. Rank Xerox management decided not to select anyone from the quality ranks for the team, because it wanted to send the message to employees that this application was being written by the entire company about the entire company. This team was ultimately responsible for compiling the data and editing the application. The team functioned smoothly because of its small size and members' experience in working as part of a team.

The first step in the team's process was to reconcile the criteria of the Rank Xerox Business Excellence Certification with the European Quality Award criteria. Although the EFQM allowed applicants to modify its criteria, the team believed that using the EFQM model of total quality was preferable because it would make it easier for the assessors to evaluate the Rank Xerox application (a good example of understanding customer requirements). The team members also reviewed the lessons learned from the Xerox Baldrige application and decided which themes and key messages they would use to address each section in the award criteria. Then the team compiled evidence from all of the Rank Xerox entities to support those messages. Every Rank Xerox country business in Europe and every site had a team that participated in data collection. Every country participated as if it was applying as an individual unit and was responsible for gathering data to support statements made in the application. Every country and site provided solid examples that were included in the application.

The team then established criteria to select what would go into the application: It examined the data for extended results over a three- to five-year period; it evaluated the results to determine whether they were clearly linked to the business processes that produced them and were strong relative to the competition or best-in-class performance; and it judged whether the results were pervasive throughout the company so that the application was not featuring an isolated example of excellence. The best examples compiled at the local level were used to build the application.

One barrier in the application process was the seventy-five-page limit for the application. The team allocated space for each section in the application according to its percentage of the total score. The application was written in anticipation of receiving a site visit. Senior executives at Rank Xerox took ownership of the various sections' content. This approach developed into section interview teams that were subsequently deployed during the site visit. The team decided to produce the application using highlight color and to print the document using only Xerox equipment. A graphics designer helped with the cover design and inserts, and external reviewers were used as editors and subject matter experts. Feedback on the application was solicited from all areas of Rank Xerox to maximize the involvement of various organizations in the self-assessment process. Xerox senior management also reviewed the document.

During the application process, Rank Xerox learned that a company's reason for applying for the award determines the strategy used for writing the application. Rank Xerox believes that if a company wants to get the most out of the award application process, it should do it honestly and involve its people.

Application summary

The Rank Xerox self-assessment presented for the European Quality Award is a refinement of the Xerox Corporation TQM approach. The following section reproduces the leadership section of the original application and, for the remaining sections, summarizes the major distinctions between the Rank Xerox quality system and the quality system contained in the Xerox Business Products and Systems application for the Baldrige Award. Both of these quality systems have a strong set of common core elements, which were developed during the 1980s as Leadership Through Quality matured into an operating philosophy for all of Xerox. The consistent use of Leadership Through Quality throughout the company is evident in the Rank Xerox application. Two major refinements featured in the Rank Xerox application are the Business Excellence Certification and policy deployment, which were implemented as a result of lessons learned from the Baldrige effort and became part of the company-wide effort for intensification of Leadership Through Quality.

---

1. LEADERSHIP

Our managers are central to the implementation of Total Quality Management. This section looks at the background of the original management decision to commit Rank Xerox to this total quality approach. It describes the training initiated and undertaken by management, the managers' use of role model behaviour, the communication of quality values and the management focus on continuous improvement to create a total quality culture.

1A VISIBLE INVOLVEMENT IN LEADING QUALITY

In the late 1970's the most senior executives in Xerox and Rank Xerox responded to aggressive and successful com-

---

petition by personally conducting a programme of bench-marking among our best competitors. The knowledge gained through this exercise unified the management of the company in the pursuit of customer satisfaction through Total Quality Management.

Against this background, our Senior Management Team developed the company Quality Policy (Figure 1.1). At the same time they developed and communicated the main elements to enable the change (Figure 1.2). The strategy by which we would implement the Quality Policy was named "Leadership Through Quality". It became first a goal; second, a strategy; and third, a process that would become the Rank Xerox way of working at all levels. Rank Xerox embarked on its Leadership Through Quality journey in 1984.

Quality Training

RANK XEROX QUALITY POLICY

"Rank Xerox is a Quality company.
Quality is the basic business principle for Rank Xerox.
Quality means providing our external and internal customers with innovative products and services that fully satisfy their requirements.
Quality improvement is the job of every employee."

Figure 1.1

ELEMENTS OF THE QUALITY STRATEGY

- Recognition and Reward
- Standards and Measures (Processes)
- Communications
- Management Behaviours and Actions
- Teamwork
- Training

Figure 1.2

Training is a manager led activity and a key opportunity for managers to communicate and demonstrate their commitment to quality. All quality training takes place in family groups and is implemented in a cascade from the top of the organisation. Rank Xerox senior management initiated the cascade by being the first group to receive training in the principles and practices of quality.

Every manager is involved twice in training: first as a member of his own manager's family group and second as the leader of his own family group. Having acquired the knowledge, skills, and processes as a member of their manager's family group, each manager then leads the training of their own family group and subsequently supports the application of quality tools and processes in the work environment. Figure 1.3 shows the extent of this activity in one of our operating units, as an example.

MANAGEMENT LED QUALITY TRAINING

Between 1984 and 1987 our French operating unit trained all 4,850 employees.

Three hundred and sixty two Quality Improvement Projects took place. The economic benefit was calculated at £1.4m.

Figure 1.3

The requirement for all managers to learn, use, teach and inspect the basic processes of Leadership Through Quality has continued, and now supports a policy that all new hires must be trained in quality within 90 days of joining the company. Whenever new work groups or departments are established, our managers use the original model of leading quality training. Progress in quality training is inspected by senior managers as an integral part of their management review process across the company.

The training plan for quality in operating units ensures that managers' skills are maintained through periodic refresher training.

The training curriculum for quality is developing to include new techniques and tools, but the pattern of training remains consistent: managers are trained first and then lead the training of their employees.

Role Model Behaviour

Each manager in Rank Xerox is expected to lead by example. This means managers must use quality tools and processes as standard management procedure in improving our processes and solving operational problems.

Senior management has developed and communicated role model manager standards. They require all managers to:

- Visibly support and promote Leadership Through Quality.

- Use and encourage the use of all quality tools.

- Use customer satisfaction as a key measure in all business decisions.

- Seek and act on feedback on their own management behaviour.

- Establish Quality plan expectations, and meet the goals set.

- Hire, develop and promote people in line with the principles of Leadership Through Quality.

- Recognise and reward people using Leadership Through Quality to achieve improved business results.

- Inspect, coach and guide people in use of quality processes.

Figure 1.4 shows a recent example of a management led team working on improvement projects.

Communication of Quality

Leadership Through Quality was first introduced to all Rank Xerox employees in 1984 in a cascade of management communication meetings. Using video and supporting documentation, the Quality Policy, strategy and key processes were explained, showing how each employee could support them.

MANAGEMENT LEADING QUALITY

In 1989-90 our German operating unit discovered through our market research activity that we were ranked number three in customer satisfaction behind Siemens and IBM in the Centralised Electronic Printing (CEP) part of our business.

In response, the German management team developed and implemented a tailored research programme to identify the causes and relative importance of the areas of dissatisfaction and how our competitors achieved their recorded satisfaction levels. Our managers visited all of our top 300 CEP customers to look for areas of improvement and to agree actions with the customers.

Following implementation of these actions our continuing research programme revealed that by 1991 we had overtaken both Siemens and IBM and gone from number three to number one in customer satisfaction.

Figure 1.4

Reinforcement of Leadership Through Quality is addressed throughout the company at monthly, quarterly and annual communications meetings (examples in Figure 1.5). The Policy Deployment process (Policy and Strategy section) is the prime way in which managers communicate quality strategy, new initiatives and changes on a continuing basis. In addition to direct management communication, each operating unit uses brochures, reference guides, posters and other media to reinforce the message.

For the last ten years our Mitcheldean plant has issued a desktop calendar to employees and suppliers, every page of which carries a quality message. Bernard Fournier, the Managing Director, issued a document called "Our Values and Direction" to Headquarters employees and senior operating unit managers. In turn they cascaded this example through their organisations. In the UK, a 50-page booklet called "Leadership Through Quality - the way we work" details the significance of quality management to the business and how each individual has a role to play. In the Netherlands we use a document called "Kwaliteit - Een Race Zonder Finish". Meeting rooms and corridors throughout the company display framed posters on quality principles and processes.

Accessibility and Listening to Staff

REINFORCEMENT OF THE QUALITY MESSAGE
(Examples)

- In our International Headquarters (IHQ)
  Bernard Fournier holds quarterly
  Communication meetings with middle
  and senior managers. The agenda always
  includes a presentation on Customer
  Satisfaction and Quality. The attendees
  of the meeting are required to cascade
  the communication to their own staffs
  and allot significant time for discussion
  and questions.

- Our Spanish operating unit has held an
  annual Quality Convention since 1985.
  The conference addresses progress and
  future plans in Leadership Through
  Quality implementation and gives public
  recognition to the efforts and successes of
  teams and individuals. A brochure of the
  conference is produced and used to
  support detailed communication to all
  employees.

Figure 1.5

Communication from employees to managers is actively fostered at Rank Xerox. All senior managers take an active part, for example Carlos Pascual in France and Vern Zelmer in the UK host regular monthly meetings with a cross section of their staff from all functions.

Bernard Fournier and the directors at International Headquarters individually host monthly "breakfast meetings" with employees. Our people have reported high satisfaction with these sessions and the practice is now widespread across Rank Xerox. At regular appraisal sessions our people also discuss general issues as well as review performance with their managers.

1B TOTAL QUALITY CULTURE

The Senior Management Committee (SMC) confirms company direction by the development and communication of annual objectives through Policy Deployment. This direction setting provides a unified set of goals for everyone in the company.

In addition to regularly providing direction, our managers

promote the use of a common set of quality tools and processes to enable our employees throughout the company to work together in pursuit of customer satisfaction. Key amongst these tools are the Problem Solving Process (PSP) (Figure 1.6) and the Quality Improvement Process (QIP) (Figure 1.7). Used pervasively and supplemented by other tools such as benchmarking, Work Process Improvement, and sharing best practices between units, they have led to major improvements in customer satisfaction and processes in all areas of our company.

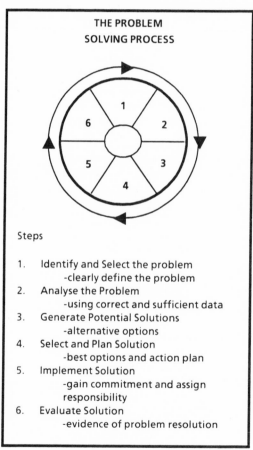

THE PROBLEM SOLVING PROCESS

Steps

1. Identify and Select the problem
   -clearly define the problem
2. Analyse the Problem
   -using correct and sufficient data
3. Generate Potential Solutions
   -alternative options
4. Select and Plan Solution
   -best options and action plan
5. Implement Solution
   -gain commitment and assign responsibility
6. Evaluate Solution
   -evidence of problem resolution

Figure 1.6

Assessing Awareness and Use of Quality

Rank Xerox managers inspect the use of tools and processes, and coach their people to ensure understanding. Participation in quality improvement activities is included in employees' individual objectives. All business proposals are required to include benchmarking data, all Quality Teams present their recommendations to the relevant management groups, and business meetings at all levels and in all parts of the company use quality tools and processes as routine. Meetings start with agreed agenda and objectives and end with formal diagnosis of what helped and hindered the achievement of objectives, to ensure that good practices are repeated and poor practices eliminated.

Appraisal of Individual Performance

The Management Resources Planning (MRP) process (People Management section) includes an evaluation of individual managers, against role model behaviours previously listed. Achievement of role model status is a prerequisite for promotion to senior management positions.

Managers review the progress of their individual employees in the use of quality, set targets for improvement and agree support plans as part of our formal appraisal process (People Management section).

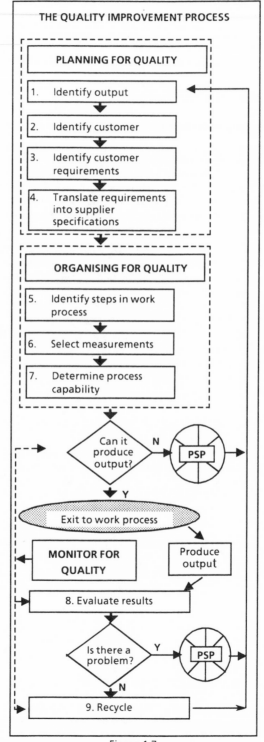

Figure 1.7

Review of Progress in Total Quality

Senior management in Rank Xerox regularly inspects the company's progress towards our goal of Leadership Through Quality, at all levels and in all functions.

At monthly and quarterly business review meetings in our operating units we measure performance against plan in each of our business priority areas. Each quarter Bernard Fournier and his headquarters directors conduct Operations Reviews with each operating unit, at which improvement opportunities and issues are reviewed. First on the agenda in all of these meetings is Customer Satisfaction, which reflects the quality that we deliver to our customers. This continuous inspection has been supplemented by a number of major reviews of our implementation of the Leadership Through Quality strategy.

Our first major assessment was conducted in 1987, three years into implementation. The review focused on the major elements of the strategy listed in Figure 1.2. As a result of this activity, the sequence of our business priorities was changed to bring Customer Satisfaction into first position, with specific improvement activities agreed and implemented.

In 1989 we conducted a further major review of progress across Rank Xerox. Building on the effectiveness of the 1987 review we increased the involvement of line managers. The outcome was the development of a Quality Intensification Plan which sharpened the focus of the original quality plan and initiated the implementation of Policy Deployment, as well as targeting improvements. In 1990 we audited progress against this plan. The audit confirmed that accelerated progress was being made and once more highlighted improvement areas. The most important of these was the establishment of Employee Motivation and Satisfaction as our second business priority. Continued self assessment of our progress in satisfying our customers through quality management led us in 1991 to the development of our Business Excellence Certification programme, described in the Policy and Strategy section, which integrates business, quality planning and review across the company.

1C RECOGNITION OF PEOPLE USING QUALITY

Recognition and Reward are key supporting tools to Leadership Through Quality, and we apply them systematically throughout the company. Recognition is given for achievement contributing to increased quality and customer satisfaction. This recognition is delivered at individual, group, departmental, national and international level, with all employees eligible.

Each of our operating units has its own approach to delivering recognition. The two schemes outlined in Figure 1.8 are typical examples; in 1991 we made awards to 20% of employees in our Venray manufacturing plant and to 13% of employees in Rank Xerox UK. The criteria and process for each scheme are communicated locally. Most awards are made publicly, and are reported in house magazines.

RECOGNITION & REWARD SCHEMES
(ascending value of award)

EUROPEAN MANUFACTURING

Individual Achievement Award
Team Achievement Award
Exceptional Performance Award
Individual Special Recognition Award
Team Excellence Award
D&M Individual Excellence Award
Presidents Award

UK OPERATING UNIT

Special Recognition Award
Team Award
Sovereign Award
Director's Award
Honours Club Award
Presidents Award

Figure 1.8

The example in Figure 1.9 represents the sort of team activity that the schemes encourage, and Figure 1.10 lists some of the ways in which our senior managers deliver recognition.

RECOGNITION OF QUALITY TEAM WORK
(MANUFACTURING)

As a result of the work of a team of six people from manufacturing, packaging changes were introduced on 13 line items. All legislation requirements were exceeded, customers reacted favourably and a saving of £1.2m was made on raw materials.

The team won an award at local level, a team certificate of achievement, and individual cash awards. It was selected to receive a Manufacturing Divisional Award, and was further selected as one of three Divisional Award Winners to go forward for a Corporate Team Excellence Award.

Figure 1.9

We consider our suppliers to be an extension of our own workforce because they impact the quality we deliver to our customers. For this reason we extend recognition of quality to our supplier base, as the examples in Figure 1.11 show.

SENIOR MANAGERS RECOGNISING QUALITY

- In Austria, Hendrik Homan the General Manager makes a Kundenphilharmoniker award every month to a person nominated by a customer for outstanding service.

- In Finland and Sweden, Rune Ericsson and Sven Olsson, the General Managers, make individual Quality Awards for outstanding contributions.

- In the Netherlands, Mike van Bachum the General Manager makes 3 awards for excellence every year.

Figure 1.10

RECOGNITION OF QUALITY SUPPLIERS

- In 1991 we held a major supplier event at our manufacturing plant in Venray, Holland. 240 individuals from 95 of our European suppliers attended. At the meeting 21 suppliers were recognised for their performance on Quality, Cost and Delivery.

- In our French operating unit an award is made each year to the transportation supplier that performs best against agreed Quality improvement targets.

Figure 1.11

Through this systematic process of public recognition of quality, we expose all our people to role model behaviour as often as possible.

1D SUPPORT FOR QUALITY THROUGH RESOURCES AND ASSISTANCE

Management demonstrates its commitment to quality through its direct personal involvement in driving and inspiring those around them and in the resources Rank Xerox makes available to support implementation.

The Quality Network

The Rank Xerox Quality Network is a major resource investment in support of line management in their implementation of quality. Each operating unit has a Quality Officer as a member of the senior management team. For example the Rank Xerox Quality Director in Headquarters is a member of the SMC. The role of this executive and all quality officers in the company is to support line management in continuous improvement of quality processes, work processes and outputs.

The Quality Director coordinates an international Quality Network, which consists of the senior Quality Officer from each operating unit. They meet every quarter and review approach, results, and new initiatives on our quality journey. They develop and recommend new policies and strategies to the SMC, and support implementation. Examples of business improvement initiatives developed by the Quality Network are shown in Figure 1.12. In addition the Quality Officer leads and coordinates the activities of a number of Quality Managers and specialists who are members of the management teams of operational functions such as sales, manufacturing, marketing and customer service. These individuals form a Quality Network in their own units. They are line managers who have received specialist training and are recognised as accomplished practitioners.

BUSINESS IMPROVEMENT DRIVEN BY THE QUALITY NETWORK

- Development of Customer Satisfaction Measurement Survey (CSMS) process in 1985.
- Process for Policy Deployment researched, developed and proposed. Implementation support provided since 1989.
- Managing By Fact (Work Process Improvement) 1990.
- Collaborative development, with senior management, of the Business Excellence Certification (BEC) Programme 1991.

Figure 1.12

Quality Officers facilitate the use of Quality processes, deliver training, help to define Quality goals and integrate quality into all management processes. The local Quality Network reviews quality projects and enables best practices to be shared amongst functions through support to line management.

Funding and Championing

Our investment in quality comprises firstly the money and manpower to train and support all our employees in the application of quality processes, and secondly the commitment of resources to implement the changes necessary to improve quality continuously.

Since 1984, we estimate that we have invested over 380 man years and spent more than £60 million in training our employees in quality. An example of funding change programmes arising from employees' use of quality processes in support of continuous improvement is given in Figure 1.13.

INVESTMENT IN QUALITY
(Example)

In 1989 a company wide QIT was formed to work on improving our software support service to customers.

This international team developed a programme of improvement which required a £3M investment in system development and an incremental headcount of 35 in our Customer Support Centres across Europe in the period 1989 - 1991.

Investment in this major programme continues with full launch scheduled for mid 1992.

Figure 1.13

Through role model behaviour, and regularly sponsoring and personally leading Quality Improvement Teams (QITs), our senior managers champion specific quality improvement activities. They call for volunteers to form QITs, agreeing the desired outputs and the timescales for the development of action plans. Once such QIT recommendations are accepted, management's task is to remove barriers to implementation.

**1E INVOLVEMENT WITH CUSTOMERS
AND SUPPLIERS**

Customers

Rank Xerox managers at all levels take every opportunity for direct involvement with customers. Direct understanding of customer requirements and customer satisfaction levels is essential to fulfillment of their role as quality managers. To support this function Executive Sponsor Programmes have been in place since the mid 1980s. Under this programme Key and Nominated customer accounts have a named senior executive at board level, who supports the Sales Account Manager.

Through a series of regular executive meetings and account reviews with such customers, our managers take the opportunity to assess our performance in meeting customer requirements with senior decision makers. All levels of Rank Xerox management are frequently involved in Customer Focus Groups as well as visits to individual customers. In operating units Product Group Marketing managers establish regular customer meetings and special interest groups.

The clear objective of these contacts is to look for areas where we can better meet the needs of our customers, by improving what we offer, or offering additional products and services.

For example, in 1989 Gunther Steffan, the Personnel Director of our Austrian operating unit, sponsored and led a QIT working on improving the telephone manner of all staff to internal and external customers. Implementation of the QIT recommendations resulted in Customer Satisfaction rating going from 73% in 1989 to 83% in 1990 and 87% in 1991.

In 1990 Manual Silva Santos, the Customer Service Director and Carlos Larramba, the Distribution Manager of our Portuguese operating unit, led a cross functional QIT to reduce abortive deliveries of equipment to customers. Against a target of 50% reduction within a year, they achieved a 60% reduction in 9 months. An example of how we use customer contacts to continuously improve our products and services is illustrated in Figure 1.14.

LISTENING TO THE PEOPLE THAT USE OUR PRODUCTS

Our operating units in Austria and Switzerland host groups of key operators from customers of our high-volume products 2 or 3 times per year and have been doing so for 4 years.

The meeting enables the customers to share views with each other and with Rank Xerox management. The meetings are also used to demonstrate new products and get customer feedback.

Figure 1.14

Suppliers

We work closely to improve quality with our suppliers throughout our operations. This has been particularly important and relevant in manufacturing where there is direct benefit to our customers and Rank Xerox through improved component and product quality.

In Germany, France and UK we use the quality processes with contractor delivery crews; in the Netherlands and UK we do the same thing with customer training contractors. We have subcontracted some 90% of our total delivery activity, but have maintained our standards for prompt and effective delivery to our customers.

In 1991 our Mitcheldean plant held a European Supplier open day, which included a session on "Continuous Supplier Involvement" (Resources section). Many of our suppliers have adopted our quality processes for their own use. Figure 1.16 provides an example of our shared approach.

WORKING WITH SUPPLIERS
(Example)

In 1987 our Norwegian operating unit introduced quality management to Hunsfoss, one of its paper suppliers.

We ran training for their management and key production workers, teaching them both QIP and PSP. As a result of a subsequent joint Quality Improvement Team we designed and produced a paper packaging that improved customer satisfaction and won the 'World Star' award in 1989 from the World Packaging Organisation.

Figure 1.16

In the UK, we have established a partnership association with suppliers of complementary products. Customers benefit from having a single point of contact, coordinated by Rank Xerox, to incorporate third party hardware, software and peripherals from many suppliers directly under a single contract. All partners' products pass a rigorous approval procedure that we set in accordance with our quality procedures. This ensures that our customers are always guaranteed a consistent high level of quality.

1F PROMOTION OF QUALITY OUTSIDE RANK XEROX

Rank Xerox management has always been active in sharing its experience and learning in quality management. The company's policy recognises the general commercial benefits that accrue from an increase in the application of quality management throughout the business communities in which it operates. Rank Xerox managers invest considerable time and effort in promoting quality management outside the company.

Professional Bodies

We are active in national and international quality organisations, both at company and individual level. Figure 1.17 lists some of our memberships. Our support for these organisations includes writing and delivering papers on specific quality topics, articles for newsletters and journals, developing and delivering seminars and regular attendance at meetings and events. A recent example was a seminar on benchmarking developed and delivered for the EFQM in Barcelona in March 1992.

RANK XEROX SUPPORT FOR QUALITY ORGANISATIONS (sample)

- British Quality Association
- Danish Society for Quality Management
- European Foundation for Quality Management (EFQM)
- Finnish Quality Association
- Spanish Quality Club
- Nederlandse Vereniging van Kwaliteitszorg
- French National Network for the promotion of Quality
- Deutsche Gesellschaft für Qualität
- Conference Board
- British Deming Association
- Portuguese National Association for Quality

Figure 1.17

Local Community

Our operating units have an Open Door policy on Quality and we are always willing to share our approach to quality management with local businesses. Senior managers from Rank Xerox frequently deliver speeches on quality management to those companies wishing to learn from our experience. We estimate that such events take place once every two weeks in our major operating units. For example Figure 1.18 lists some of the many companies and local government organisations that have taken the opportunity to learn from our experience in the UK.

SHARING THE PRINCIPLES OF QUALITY
UK EXAMPLES

- Woolwich Building Society
- Equity & Law
- East Sussex County Council
- BP International HQ
- Ford Motor Company
- National Westminster Bank
- Mercury Communications
- British Rail
- Texaco
- Hertfordshire County Council
- Unisys Limited
- Ferranti International
- British Telecom
- IBM

Figure 1.18

Conferences and Seminars

Our top managers are personally involved in presenting on Leadership Through Quality. In September 1991 Bernard Fournier spoke at a senior management forum at Renault; Steve Tierney (then head of Manufacturing) presented on benchmarking at a major conference held by the Institute of International Research in Germany in October 1991; Vern Zelmer regularly hosts Quality days in the UK with customers and suppliers.

We often work to improve quality in practice by helping national and local governments. In Denmark, Mogens Nielsen, our Quality officer, is working with the Danish Management Centre to develop a Danish Quality Award whilst Flemming Norklit, the General Manager, has worked with the Government Data Department (Data Centralen) on the concepts of Total Quality Management.

Books and Articles

Rank Xerox managers and quality officers have written many articles on the theory and practice of quality management, some examples of which are listed in Figure 1.19. The company has regularly encouraged its people to be quoted, and the company's experience used, in management journals and publications concerned with quality. The extent and effectiveness of Rank Xerox's efforts to promote quality management are reflected in the extent to which the company is referenced in text books on the subject and featured in press articles.

EXAMPLES OF PUBLICATIONS

- The Role of the Manager   J Verkerk
- Benchmarking   B Rogers
- Management Revolution   R Walker
- Quality in our work &   F Musch &
  Organisation   P Halink

Figure. 1.19

SOLVING PROBLEMS TOGETHER

In Austria we hold an annual customer satisfaction review meeting with our transport and delivery contractors.

At the meeting our 7 suppliers work together using the Problem Solving Process, led by a Rank Xerox manager, to develop action plans to improve customer satisfaction areas under their control.

Figure 1.15

2. POLICY AND STRATEGY

- Rank Xerox strategies depend on the influences of the European market. The "European Dimension" strategy describes the approach to customer support, research and development, sourcing, marketing, and distribution in Europe. It was based on an analysis of European Economic Community trends and benchmarked against DEC, Olivetti, Apple, and other high-technology companies.

- Since 1989, Rank Xerox has used policy deployment as the annual process for turning strategic direction into operational business plans. Policy deployment is designed around the quality principles of customer requirements, people involvement, negotiated and agreed common objectives, management control that accommodates local empowerment within the operating units, and the regular self-assessment of performance as an input to plan renewal.

- Policy deployment creates a hierarchy of priorities, objectives, and vital few actions. It is cascaded through each operating unit, where it becomes the framework for the development of its objectives and activities.

- This cascade process means that individuals have clear personal direction and targets, can relate their activities to other people, and understand how to contribute to the success of the company. At the level of the individual, the assessment against plan takes the form of a personal appraisal as part of our people management practices.

A document is produced annually in all of our operating units to support and reinforce the communication of policy deployment. In the Rank Xerox headquarters, it is known as the Blue Book, but it has different local titles in different operating units. This document contains the quality policy, values and direction, mission statement and strategy, in addition to company, unit, and functional objectives.

- Business Excellence Certification (BEC) is a company-wide, uniform process to assess progress toward each of the forty elements that provide an operational definition of Leadership Through Quality. The self-assessment by each management team is then validated by trained, senior line managers from other units.

- Achieving certification under the BEC program means that a Rank Xerox operating unit has demonstrated an operational command of Leadership Through Quality tools and processes, is achieving good business results characterized by continuous improvement, and has demonstrated good prevention-based processes throughout the organization.

3. PEOPLE MANAGEMENT

- Employee motivation and satisfaction was established as a corporate priority in 1989. In 1990, it was ranked second only to customer satisfaction. Rank Xerox reinforced the emphasis on its people by introducing a formal measurement of employee satisfaction and a closed-loop measurement process.

- Objective-setting and appraisal processes have been in place throughout Rank Xerox since the 1970s and are based on discussions and agreements between the individual and his or her manager. In 1990, Rank Xerox integrated the policy deployment process for cascading company objectives with the process of setting individual objectives. As a result, individuals can see how their objectives relate to department, function, operating unit, and company-wide objectives.

- All employees are involved in contributing to continuous improvement and quality through the process of objective-setting and its linkage to policy deployment.

- Appraisal activities are synchronized with objective-setting and identification of Employee Development Action plans, resulting in a closed-loop process.

4. RESOURCES

- Rank Xerox prepares its financial plans in line with the priorities and direction given through the policy deployment process. In particular, it considers investment in products, market share, and customer satisfaction to ensure that its quality and business objectives are supported in the most effective manner.

- Rank Xerox uses the concept of Cost of Quality to focus awareness on the costs of nonconformance. In-process measures focus on defect prevention and improved operating efficiencies.

- Information Technology (IT) investments are reviewed to assess their impact on the four business priorities (customer satisfaction, employee satisfaction, market share, and Return On Assets). The IT strategy is based on application systems and technology. Application development is driven by business processes and is divided into three areas: customer processes, core process systems, and the product delivery process.

5. PROCESSES

- When Rank Xerox first implemented Leadership Through Quality in 1984, it focused on process identification and improvement. As Rank Xerox became more familiar with the Quality Improvement Process (QIP) at the work level, it applied the process to large-scale functional processes and later moved into cross-functional and cross-organizational processes. This progression enabled the definition of the full Business Architecture in 1990. This is an integrated process structure which describes all the process areas that make up the business and includes process detail for seventy-six subprocesses. This Business Architecture is the template for future process and systems development. The three macro-level processes of the Business Architecture are the customer interface process, the logistics process, and the Product Delivery Process (PDP).

- Process ownership is based on the outputs of a process which are needed to meet a particular mission where the output supplier takes process responsibility, applies QIP and its accompanying quality tools to ensure that processes are under control, and ensures that their output meets the customer's requirements.

- Performance measurement is the key to effective process management. Having established standards with the customer, the process owner defines the measures needed for effective control, either in-process or as a summary of process capability.

- In-process measurement and review of performance enable appropriate action to be taken before control limits are exceeded. The use of fact-based measures for process management provides the data needed to run the business and identifies opportunities for improvement.

- A process-tiered measurement system is used to set targets and measure performance for policy deployment objectives from the top management level to the level of individual employees.

- Business Excellence Certification (BEC) provides the means for business process assessment from the viewpoint of the customer. BEC starts with Leadership Through Quality and the vision of Rank Xerox as a total quality company, and encompasses a forty-item self-assessment. Rank Xerox trained thirty-eight senior managers to conduct their own self-assessment ratings and 105 internal examiners to conduct the validation activities.

6. CUSTOMER SATISFACTION

- Customer satisfaction is the highest business priority of Rank Xerox. The goal is to be rated first in customer satisfaction for all reprographic and printing products in all European countries by the end of 1992 and to achieve 100 percent customer satisfaction by the end of 1993.

- When Rank Xerox set these goals, they were supported by a strategy that had been in place for five years and continuously developed over that time. Customer satisfaction was established as the principal business priority in 1987 and a Customer Satisfaction Measurement System

(CSMS) was established. In 1988, bonuses were paid based on CSMS results, an industry first. In 1990, policy deployment was introduced to provide clear, consistent direction on goals, targets, and actions throughout Rank Xerox. A "closed-loop" measurement, analysis, and action process was developed for customer satisfaction. In 1991, the BEC process was introduced to assess all key business factors from the customer's perspective.

- The closed-loop process has been used to identify and understand the root causes of customer dissatisfaction, and action plans have been developed to improve performance in these areas.

- In January 1991, Rank Xerox launched a Total Satisfaction Guarantee as an expression of confidence in its products, services, and processes. Under this guarantee, the customer can obtain an exchange for any product with which he or she is not fully satisfied, within three years of purchase. During the first year of the guarantee program, less than 0.5 percent of Rank Xerox customers have used the guarantee.

7. PEOPLE SATISFACTION

- As part of the closed-loop management process, all operating units communicate their employee satisfaction survey results to all employees. The units establish QITs and conduct root cause analysis before making recommendations for improvements. This process is used for continuous improvement even if the results are above national norms.

8. IMPACT ON SOCIETY

- Rank Xerox is proactive in its concern to safeguard the environment. Throughout the 1980s, Rank Xerox implemented improved standards, which exceeded legal requirements, wherever possible. Key improvement areas have been energy conservation, waste disposal, elimination of waste, ozone depletion, and recycling materials.

- The Rank Xerox policy on environmental health and safety drives responsible action by the company throughout all units.

- In addition to numerous ISO 9000 certifications, Rank Xerox units have received sixteen major quality awards since 1983.

9. BUSINESS RESULTS

- Market share has improved over forty percent since 1986, when loss of market share to competition was halted.

- Return on assets has been stable and consistently better than the United Kingdom upper quartile for this industry over the past three years.

- Over the past three years, productivity in Unit Manufacturing Cost has averaged 4.8 percent annually.

- In 1991, over fifty percent of all manufacturing processes achieved a Cpk greater than 1.33, which indicates that 99.994 percent of the process output is within specification limits. Rank Xerox has set a goal to have more than seventy percent of its processes controlled to exceed this level by the end of 1992.

Board of Examiners feedback report summary

Like the Baldrige Award process, each applicant for the European Quality Award receives a feedback report from the assessors. The feedback report summarizes the findings of the assessors and reports strengths and areas for improvement for each of the award criteria. The following is a summary of the 1992 Rank Xerox feedback report.

Summary report
In 1992, approximately thirty applications were filed for the first European Quality Award and, of these, fewer than one-third received site visits. (Specific numbers for applicants and site visits have not been released by the EFQM.) Of the companies that received site visits, four received the 1992 European Quality Prize: British Oxygen Company, Milliken, Ubisa (a subsidiary of Bekaert), and Rank Xerox. (Milliken also won the Baldrige Award in 1989 with Xerox.) In October, Rank Xerox was named the first recipient of the European Quality Award.

While the exact score of a company's application is not reported to the applicant, a range is reported. The feedback report stated that the Rank Xerox application scores were in the range of 701 to 800 points of the total 1000 points, with a particular strength noted in policy and strategy. The assessors commented in the summary statement from the feedback report: "The company has clearly embraced the quality process in order to overcome serious threats to its survival and has recovered much of its former position in the marketplace. The general impression is of a company with a clear policy for the pursuit of excellence."

In addition to the overall comments and score, each applicant receives a detailed description of areas of strength and areas for improvement. The following paragraphs provide the detailed observations by the assessors of the Rank Xerox application.

> *It is interesting to observe the cultural differences between the feedback reports provided for the Baldrige Award application and the European Quality Award application. The European Quality Award feedback report, in general, is more detailed and reflects the increasing expectations of examiners as standards of excellence increase overtime.*
>
> **1. Leadership**
>
> *Strengths*
>
> - The Quality Policy and elements of the Quality Strategy have been developed and communicated by the Senior Management Team.
>
> - Quality training is led by managers, and they are expected to train "family group" members.
>
> - There is a strong top-down approach led by the chief executive.
>
> - Role model standards have been set by the senior managers.
>
> - The Total Quality culture is continually reinforced through the use of a consistent set of quality tools and problem solving processes throughout the company.
>
> - Managers are evaluated against role model behavior, and achievement of role model status is a prerequisite for promotion.
>
> - All business proposals are required to include benchmarking data.
>
> - Meetings at all levels start with an agreed agenda and objectives, and are evaluated at the end.

- Recognition in the form of awards for achievement of increased quality and customer satisfaction are given at the individual, group, departmental, national, and international level.

- In some cases, award winners are nominated by customers.

- Recognition is extended outside the company to suppliers.

- Each operating unit has a Quality Officer and, together with the Quality Director in Headquarters, they form the Quality Network.

- This Quality Network initiates and develops business improvements.

- The Quality Officers deliver training in their own units and form local Quality Networks.

- Over 380 man-years and £60 million have been invested in training since 1984.

- There is a well-established Executive Sponsor program for nominated board-level executives to support Sales Account Managers.

- All levels of managers are involved with customers through customer focus groups.

- There is a process for working with suppliers to solve problems together, and the company provides training for suppliers.

- There is active support and involvement in Quality organizations throughout Europe, and the company's managers invest considerable time and effort in promoting Quality Management outside the company.

- There is a high degree of involvement with other companies and local businesses to share experiences of Total Quality.

- Company staff have published several books and articles on the theory and practice of Quality Management.

- Lectures on aspects of quality are given at conferences and seminars by all management levels from the Chief Executive down.

Areas for Improvement

- Communication on quality by the most senior management

appears confined to formal sessions, and direct communication with staff at their place of work could be increased.

- Deployment of the quality culture did not reach to the lowest levels of staff.

- The "Blue Book" did not penetrate as far down the line as management planned or believed.

- Awareness and knowledge of quality tools and techniques was not apparent at the lowest levels.

- The recognition system was very formal and management-controlled. Staff were not empowered to make more spontaneous and informal rewards for quality achievement.

- There was no evidence of evaluation and review of the effectiveness of the award system.

- Supplier awards appear to be confined to certain classes of operation only. Eligibility should be extended.

- There is no benchmark data against which to judge training resource allocation, e.g., training costs as percent of budget or man-days of training per employee.

- There is no trend data on money or resources devoted to Quality Support.

- Except in isolated circumstances, there is no evidence of "partnership" with customers.

- There is no trend data with respect to customer visits or supplier involvement.

- There is no evidence of regular review cycles to measure the effectiveness of the involvement with customers and suppliers.

- Although the company's involvement in spreading the quality message is considerable, the degree to which this is based on a systematic, rather than an ad hoc approach, is unclear.

2. Policy and Strategy

Strengths

- The company's values are clearly based on TQM principles and strongly customer-driven.

- There is clear evidence of the review and refinement of the values over the years.

- There is a sound, systematic approach to determining customer needs and using this as a source for strategy and policy determination.

- Benchmarking is used extensively in all areas of the business.

- External and societal trends are considered in strategy development.

- There is an annual policy deployment process directly linking values and vision through strategy into vital few actions and individual targets.

- New policies and strategies are often piloted before implementation.

- Many forms of communication are used within the company. The major means of communication for policies and strategies is through the involvement of all staff in the objective-setting cycle.

- All employees receive a document including quality policy values and direction, mission statements, and strategy each year.

- Employees evaluate the clarity of the communication through questionnaires, supplemented by question-and-answer sessions.

- The effectiveness and relevance of the company's policy is measured from the results of systematic customer surveys.

- The introduction of the Business Excellence Certification process has resulted in a company-wide, uniform process for self-assessment.

- There is continuous appraisal of performance of six major elements of the business and forty subelements.

Areas for Improvement

- Although the company is involved with suppliers to a high degree, the values do not include the company's commitment to its suppliers.

- The incorporation of employee inputs into the strategy does not appear to be carried out in a structured manner.

- The degree to which the policy deployment process is reviewed and evaluated is unclear.

- The approach is heavily "top-down" and the degree to which the "bottom-up" process can influence the policies is not clear.

- The approach to communicating policy and strategy is excellent, but based on the level of awareness of staff tested on the site visits, the deployment needs to be increased at the lower levels of the organization.

- There is no evidence that attendance at communications meetings (measured as a percentage of the total staff) is increasing or decreasing.

- The Business Excellence Certification process is a relatively recent introduction and, as yet, there is no evidence of its effectiveness.

- The degree to which feedback from employees is incorporated into the process is unclear.

3. People Management

Strengths

- There is a well-developed, systematic approach to the selection, training, and development of the company's managers and future managers.

- Since 1990, there have been regular employee satisfaction surveys at all sites.

- Employee satisfaction has been incorporated as the number two business priority after customer satisfaction.

- Managers are evaluated annually against five key criteria.

- Long-term skills requirements are identified through the three- to five-year planning and long-range strategic planning process.

- There is an employee development policy in place and employees are involved in planning their own development.

- There is a comprehensive package of specific operational skills training with standard requirements for both the type and timing of training.

- Training effectiveness is measured in several ways, including via the customer survey.

- There is a well-developed process for objective-setting and agreeing on individual targets. This process is linked with the company objectives through the policy deployment process.

- The performance levels against which achievement of the objectives will be measured are established and agreed upon by the manager and employee.

- The objective-setting cycle has been developed regularly since its inception in the 1970s.

- Employee suggestion programs have operated in the United Kingdom for many years and now have been extended to all locations.

- There is an extended culture of using Quality Improvement Teams. These have expanded from "family groups" operation to national and international processes.

- There is a common language of quality through the use of common principles.

- The employee satisfaction survey shows high scores for teamwork.

Areas for Improvement

- Policies for development of staff below the manager level are unclear.

- The views of employees on Performance Evaluation are variable with two countries scoring below fifty percent satisfied.

- The link between HR plans and business needs is unclear.

- There is no numerical trend data for training performed year-to-year.

- Overall satisfaction with training is approximately sixty percent. The use which is made of the training effectiveness measurements to improve this rating is unclear.

- Although there has been an increase in the percentage of employees satisfied with the appraisal system, this satisfaction level is only seventy percent.

- The degree to which the development of the objective-setting cycle has been based on systematic evaluation, with improvements based on objective evidence, is unclear.

- It is unclear how many people participate in the suggestion programs and, apart from one location, there is no trend data.

- Although approximately sixty percent of employees are involved in QITs at any one time, there is no trend data to show whether this percentage is increasing or declining.

- The emphasis in the suggestion programs appears to be on cost savings rather than customer satisfaction.

- The extent of empowerment and how employees are empowered is unclear.

4. Resources

Strengths

- There is a clear focus on improving the net worth of the company with clear plans for investment and growth.

- Financial plans are prepared in line with the priorities and direction given through the policy deployment process.

- Cash management is benchmarked against leading corporate treasury departments.

- There is a closed-loop process to allow variances in profit, debtors, inventory, and capital spend to be analyzed for impact on cash requirements and to follow up with corrective action.

- There is already a high degree of database integration, and the company's objective is to achieve 100 percent integration.

- The IT strategies are reviewed at the operating unit level and ratified by the Information Management Board. Strategy elements are reviewed against the four business priorities.

- Database systems are used widely in the company, and information is readily available to all staff.

- Billing quality has shown improvement toward the ninety-eight percent accuracy target.

- The company has developed the Continuous Supplier Involvement process. This includes full partnership, the provision of training and support, participation in design, and a recognition process.

- There are regular reviews of this CSI process in-house and with suppliers.

- The supplier base has been reduced worldwide from 5,000 to 414 over an eleven-year period.

- Inventory management has cut inventory in half, as measured by Days of Supply.

- There is a well-defined process for evaluating new and emerging technologies against the company vision and five key criteria.

- The Bushey Data Centre is the UK benchmark for service level and cost.

- Technology built into products has resulted in a number of world "firsts."

Areas for Improvement

- The breadth of use and review of Cost of Quality across the group is unclear.

- The use of internal benchmarking is mentioned, but there is little evidence of its use.

- The degree to which the cash management process is reviewed and improved is unclear.

- The use of IT seems to be confined within the company. There is no evidence of extending its use to customers and suppliers; e.g., through EDI, automatic customs clearance, et cetera.

- The extent to which data accuracy is monitored and improved is unclear.

- The inventory reduction process appears to have stalled over the past two years.

- The degree to which involvement of suppliers and inventory management is benchmarked against best practice is unclear.

- The cost effectiveness of the use of technology in the company is unclear.

- The degree to which the process of evaluating new technologies is reviewed and improved is unclear.

5. Processes

Strengths

- Key processes are defined through customer requirements based on full Business Architecture.

- Subprocesses are defined from key processes.

- Key processes have been evolved through benchmarking and sharing internal best practices.

- Regular meetings of process owners are used to address and resolve interface issues.

- Process ownership is vested with the output supplier and the process owner defines the standards of operation against a standard checklist.

- Process monitoring is carried out at two levels—at each process step against defined standards and for the complete process.

- Performance measures are the key to the effective management of the process. They are designed in a tiered way to match policy deployment objectives.

- There is regular monitoring through management review.

- The QIP and PSP, which run through the corporate approach to quality, contain steps for managing the implementation of change and evaluating benefits.

- Responsibility for key change activities such as communicating, training, and setting success criteria, rests with the process owner.

- Changes with company-wide potential are piloted.

- The Business Excellence Certification process is being used to assist change.

- There is a strong customer satisfaction measurement system, with each operating unit having a customer satisfaction manager.

- Supplier feedback is obtained through the continuous supplier involvement process.

- There are regular reviews of processes.

- Benchmarking is applied to activities related to key processes.

- Both in-house and independent customer surveys are used.

- There is a strong "improvement culture," which has been developed over several years based on training, QITs, and the Quality Improvement Process.

- The company operates formal suggestion programs throughout its operating units.

- There is a recognition and reward system.

- Innovative and creative skills are recruitment criteria for certain areas of the business.

Areas for Improvement

- The process for review and improvement of the support processes is not clear.

- The ISO 9000 certification process is not complete for all countries.

- There is no data yet on sustained performance measurement and improvement.

- The extent to which the company implements process changes and evaluates the benefit outside the manufacturing and development area is unclear.

- The processes for prioritizing and funding the process improvements are not clear.

- There is no evidence that the sharing of knowledge of internal best practices is carried out systematically.

- There is no evidence of how the process for stimulating innovation and creativity is assessed and improved.

- There is no trend data on the number of suggestions, the percent of staff making suggestions, or the number involved in QITs to assess whether this is increasing or diminishing.

6. Customer Satisfaction

Strengths

- Customer satisfaction parameters are generated down to a

great level of detail to allow the development of specific measures.

- The targets set are ambitious.

- Overall customer satisfaction is high, and the company has a high rating when compared with most competitors.

- The trends are generally positive, although adverse trends are apparent in one or two countries.

- Adverse trends are being addressed.

- The company has developed and implemented a policy of unconditional guarantee of exchange.

Areas for Improvement

- Two countries had low overall satisfaction scores in 1991.

- There is considerable variation of performance over the past four years—improvement has not been continuous.

7. People Satisfaction

Strengths

- Overall employee satisfaction has increased in most operating units.

- Satisfaction targets have been met in thirteen out of fifteen countries.

- QITs have been established to address areas of low scoring in the satisfaction survey. These are led by directors and senior managers.

- There has been a relatively high response rate to the survey.

Areas for Improvement

- Two countries had overall satisfaction scores of approximately fifty percent, and scores were low overall.

- National norm data shows four out of nine operating units below their national norms.

- The employee satisfaction survey showed a clear distinction in satisfaction levels between the highest and lowest grades, with lower grades being significantly less satisfied.

- Absenteeism data appears to be collected only for manufacturing sites. It should be extended to all operations.

- Indirect satisfaction measures do not appear to be benchmarked.

8. Impact on Society

Strengths

- The company has a clear health, safety, and environmental policy, which has been extended to include the community at large.

- In manufacturing, the company has achieved an incident rate better than the benchmark.

- Product designs have been developed to cut dust and noise emissions to well below industry standards.

- Through the development of business parks, donations, and time, the company has supported work creation schemes.

- The company provides extensive support to employees involved with local organizations through matching fund raising, time off, et cetera.

Areas for Improvement

- There does not appear to be any benchmark data for the company's activity in this area, with the exception of safety incidents.

- It is not clear the extent to which the company's considerable effort in this area is systematic and planned.

- There is no trend data on the number of people involved with the community and the levels of expenditures.

9. Business Results

Strengths

- The company has consistently delivered against planned profits and, in general, profits have increased.

- Return On Assets has consistently been better than the industry upper quartile.

- Market share trends have been good.

- The company is the benchmark for the management of debtors.

- There are positive trends on nonfinancial areas such as cycle time, delivery, and quality.

Areas for Improvement

- There is no evidence of improvement trends in overhead or marketing costs, and no benchmark data on these measures.

- There are no benchmarks of financial performance against similar companies.

Another milestone — another challenge

The application for the European Quality Award, like the Baldrige Award application, provided an opportunity for Xerox to learn about itself and to gain a unique, external perspective on its operations. These "interventions" in the normal business cycle not only challenge the way business is conducted, but also provide an opportunity to build enthusiasm for increased efforts to improve quality and productivity. The Rank Xerox experience has provided an additional calibration point for the continued journey of Xerox employees, suppliers, and partners toward world-class levels of customer delight. The challenge of continued commitment, learning, growth, and performance will be met by a renewed emphasis on Leadership Through Quality.

Chapter Seven
Documenting the Journey

It takes perspective and maturity to learn difficult lessons. Xerox learned by reviewing its actions and experiences over the past ten to fifteen years. The lessons described in this chapter were critical to understanding, maintaining, and improving the business health of the company. The lessons confirmed the importance of continuing to support Leadership Through Quality in all of the company's activities.

Unwavering senior support is essential

It is often said that Total Quality Management cannot be effectively deployed across an enterprise without the visible leadership of a senior manager or management team that vigorously practices TQM processes and behaviors.

Xerox experiences, worldwide, indicate that senior management's visible practice of TQM principles and processes is required. It is mandatory to have a proactive senior management team that has a solid understanding of the TQM approach and has internalized its fundamental principles; believes that TQM ensures success; and is committed to assuring implementation of TQM throughout the company. Senior management must select the right people to develop and implement TQM plans—management teams who will be TQM role models—and provide them with unwavering support. Senior managers should reinforce positive efforts by seeking out, encouraging, developing and rewarding practitioners of TQM. The persistent, open communication of internal success stories by senior management provides a powerful incentive for the resistant areas within the company to move ahead in their TQM journey.

Because they have assigned implementation to role model managers and have empowered them to act, members of the senior management team do not need to be statistical experts in TQM methods. However, they **do** need to maintain their fluency in the fundamentals of quality methods; senior management cannot take a passive role—allowing it to happen or merely accepting the results that are presented without a critical assessment of the process. As David Kearns once said: "Quality is not a spectator sport." Senior managers must be more like a player-coach—not just watching the game, but able to give advice, training tips, or even step in when the team is floundering and needs a spark of executive participation in a more personal way.

The implementation team must use TQM tools with confidence and must believe that senior management will support its mission. This team will deploy the training, inspect the use of processes, and use TQM tools in practice. They will draw fishbone diagrams and will lead brainstorming sessions. They will pursue problems to their root cause. They will lead by example. The example is that of a role model manager who will insist on fact-based decisions. In Xerox, this type of leadership behavior is based on the phrase, "you can expect what you inspect." Inspecting means the use of diagnostic questions to probe for the depth of deployment of quality methods. For instance:

- Who is the customer for this output?
- What are the customer's requirements for this output?
- How will you know when you have met those requirements?
- How will you measure the capability of your process to consistently deliver the desired output?

Asking questions like these represents a key element in leading by example.

Visible, vocal, and frequent communication by senior management is invaluable to the implementation teams. Senior management's key responsibility is to inspect for enforcement of TQM practices and principles. Senior managers must continually ask the right questions to ensure that the TQM strategy is being followed. In order to inspect the processes, the processes must be understood. With inspection, managers continuously improve their understanding of TQM. The teams being inspected receive encouragement, recognition, and instruction. Word spreads quickly that the senior leaders are serious about TQM, and deployment of this desired management behavior follows more quickly.

Inspection by managers throughout the organization should send the message that quality is not negotiable. Any break in the chain will cause the practice of TQM to atrophy. If a manager is diligent in inspection, a non-practicing subordinate will not be tolerated. If an exception is made, the subordinates of the non-TQM person will lack coaching and support. When the group involved faces stress and disappointment on the job, it will lack the necessary encouragement and support. When it achieves success, it will not receive the recognition it deserves for using TQM. Over time, decay of the TQM system is inevitable.

Clearly, senior management team must also demonstrate its obsession with and passion for customer satisfaction. TQM is based on the principle that understanding customer requirements and satisfying them is why a business exists. Customer satisfaction can only be achieved by informed, committed, empowered people striving for continuous improvement. A manager who supports TQM must support the people who deliver customer satisfaction.

Getting customer and supplier feedback is necessary
As TQM is implemented, teams often get their responsibilities confused. Everyone is eager to contribute. First-line workers undertake substantial restructuring projects, and senior teams take on operationally minute ones. It is important that each level of management seek improvement in domains where it has the power, vision, and process capability to successfully implement proposed changes.

First-line employees should spend most of their time using Total Quality Management processes and systems that produce the fundamental outputs of the business. A portion of their time should be dedicated to improving their processes. They should be asking their immediate customers (the people who receive their output), "How am I doing?"; "What can I do to better satisfy your needs?" They should be engaging their suppliers to improve the work that they receive. They should be saying, "If you could change this, it would make the quality of my output better." If the first-line team has innovative ideas for more change, it should communicate these ideas to management. Management should provide immediate acknowledgement, rapid processing, and thoughtful feedback.

Middle managers should spend most of their time soliciting employee feedback that will enable them to support the processes and improvements undertaken by their teams. They should be asking the other groups, departments, or end customers who receive their department's output, "How are we doing? What can we do better?" They should be seeking improvements from their group's suppliers. They should be sharing information with their employee teams and seeking counsel from them. If the middle manager has an idea for a breakthrough change, he or she should complete the necessary research and submit the idea to senior management. Senior management should immediately acknowledge receipt of the proposal and work with the submitter to review it.

Breakthrough changes, such as 10X changes or process reengineering, are the responsibility of senior management. Senior managers should be examining fact-based analyses and seeking areas where breakthrough changes will provide the most benefit to the business. Senior management should assign teams to pursue these vital few breakthrough candidates and should provide adequate resources for them. The majority of senior management's time should be spent doing the work of leadership—guiding the business, ensuring financial strength, and acting as the "visionary" and the "banker." Senior management should not waste time meddling in the work of others. Only the senior management team has the information and authority to direct the course of the business. If the leaders are occupied in the workplace critiquing daily operations, who will perform the vital role of senior management?

Everyone in the organization, including the "top of the house", can use the quality tools to enhance the business. Some must focus on operations and small daily improvements. Some must support the workers and focus on process modification. Others must guide the business and support dramatic change.

Empowerment: A natural outgrowth of TQM

The concept of empowerment is a natural outgrowth of employee involvement and TQM that has received a great deal of management attention in the past decade. Empowerment refers to teams or individuals who have been given appropriate training or coaching, have an excellent knowledge of their processes and responsibilities, have access to needed information and data, and perform their duties with relatively little direction. All of these activities are in direct support of their customers.

A truly empowered organization is built upon an environment where there is trust and trustworthiness. An environment where the value system encourages interdependence–a win-win relationship between employees and managers where management behavior that is consistent with beliefs allows individuals to apply their creativity and ingenuity to solve business problems in an atmosphere of acceptance and with a growing sense of self-esteem. Fear has no place in such an environment. Such a working environment can have a positive influence on productivity because empowered workers are more willing to fully engage and involve themselves in their work processes. But empowerment is a relatively recent management concept and the examples of successful implementations are scarce. Caution in implementation is warranted because empowerment requires a significant shift in behaviors. There are two major challenges to empowerment: the managers who feel their positions are threatened and the workers who are to be held accountable for decisions and business results.

It is logical and understandable that managers who have worked hard to achieve the title of "manager," who have risen from the ranks of those getting direction to those giving it, are reluctant to give up decision-making power. Worse yet, they are being asked to coach their people to enable them to act without daily direction, thus, in effect, eliminating their own jobs.

It is also understandable (nevertheless a surprise) that workers, when given power to act independently, tend not to exercise it. There are fears on the part of management that workers will "go wild" and act rashly and imprudently. The Xerox experience is quite the opposite. Often employees who are conditioned to receiving daily direction and accustomed to acting without responsibility for failed initiatives ("I'm only acting on orders.") tend, when turned loose, to wait for direction. Part of a traditional manager's job involves accepting the anxiety for potential failure. If empowerment is taken to the limit of its academic definition, then this anxiety is transferred to the worker. For instance, the stress associated with recruiting a replacement worker would now fall on the empowered team, rather than upon the manager.

Clearly, there are major benefits to having empowered people. They are closest to the action, most knowledgeable about operations details, and can act and react quickly. Management overhead is reduced. The time required for response to critical business issues decreases. Employee motivation increases. These benefits are great enough to warrant continued pursuit of the empowerment concept. It must, however, be approached thoughtfully and carefully. Because empowerment is a relatively new management practice, we do not yet have the necessary knowledge to facilitate its rapid adoption. There are many issues, such as career development and compensation, that need to effectively evolve into established practice. In particular, the paradox associated with "how do we get managers to coach themselves out of jobs" has to be addressed.

Here the plan, do, check, act cycle has helped.

As Xerox tries to define and implement empowerment, it begins to focus on an operational definition of empowerment described in the context of Deming's "red bead" experiment. The red bead experiment illustrates that a system with inherent defects (red beads) must be changed by managerial action. Xerox learned that empowered teams have the enablers and freedom to refine their work processes in a way that will help them to get fewer red beads (which represent defects) out of the box. The alternative is to spend money, effort, and time, only to push red beads around inside the box without making any meaningful change in the outcome of the work process. A key point is to think of the concept of empowerment in terms of outputs of the team or the process.

The soft stuff is the hard stuff

Paul Allaire coined the phrase, "the soft stuff is the hard stuff." He realized that any change in organizational structure and process would be relatively easy to plan and implement compared to changes in behavior.

Remember that when Xerox began to deploy the ideas of empowerment throughout the company, it faced two major behavioral challenges: one from those managers who would be eliminated as the company shifted from a people-to-process focus, and one from the workers who would be held accountable to produce improved process results.

The advice of behavioral scientists and specialists can be useful for companies attempting such widespread behavioral change. The knowledge that Xerox gained comes largely from ten years of practical experience supported by David Nadler and Delta Consulting.

Behavior change can be handled in the same manner as any other desired result. Basically, the desired state must be described in terms that will allow the audience to understand and internalize "how we will act when we get there." The current state needs to be assessed. A perception survey that communicates peer and subordinate views about managers' behavior is an excellent assessment tool. A gap analysis, comparing the desired state to the current state, will point to the vital few areas most in need of improvement. Action plans can then be put in place to focus on the vital few.

These plans must encompass all aspects of the "system" that constitute behavior. "System" elements, such as rewards and recognition, training, and standards and measures, must be modified to align with the desired behaviors. If communication of the desired state is all that is done, the system will reject the behavior change.

It is important for the senior management team to be among the first to embark on the behavior change. They will be observed closely by their subordinates. Are they "walking like they talk"? They should be urged to personally communicate the desired state to as many audiences as possible. This process reinforces the desired-state behaviors in the senior managers, heightens their understanding of the concepts, and makes the required behaviors more visible. Emphasis should be placed on the inadequacies of the "old behavior" in order to make the transition to the new state more desirable.

The challenge of behavioral change was typified in the Xerox efforts to adopt an obsession with customer satisfaction, moving away from behaviors that were solely focused on financial return, even to the exclusion of customer needs. The desired state—a balanced set of priorities, with the customer number one, employees number two, and business results number three—was developed and continuously communicated through a broad range of communication vehicles. The seriousness of the current state was made vivid in videotapes showing Xerox customers castigating Xerox practices and procedures. Once the need for change was understood, then improvements could be made. Reward, recognition, and promotion systems were modified. Training programs were implemented. All essential "system" elements were addressed and aligned. A change agent, a vice president of quality and customer satisfaction, was announced and empowered. The result? In 1990, ninety-seven percent of Xerox employees felt that Xerox considered the customer the number one priority. Customer satisfaction results show Xerox to be the benchmark worldwide. A unique, bold total satisfaction guarantee, effective worldwide, was announced in 1990. A remarkable turnaround!

Alignment: Lost but making good time

In any business, it is important to ensure that goal alignment is achieved. Basically, all parties should understand the end point or vision and should be working toward common goals. The challenge is magnified as the number of players increases. The difficulty is geometrically increased when the players are grouped into functional cells.

Over time, in a larger business, a lack of alignment may result in a diffused organizational response to the business goals. Entry-level people, first-line employees, may not be able to articulate the business goals, much less explain how they will contribute to the achievement of them. Furthermore, each group in an organization tends to develop its favorite projects or programs, and these may not contribute to senior management's goals. Individuals then add their own favorite tasks, and the workload exceeds the process capability to deliver all of these commitments. As a result, either all tasks get anemic support and produce, at best, mediocre results, or personal favorites get the focus to the detriment of activities that might better serve the entire business.

Communication of goals is not enough. The business needs a structural process that starts with defined long-term goals that have measures. Xerox calls this process "managing for results" in the United States and "policy deployment" in Europe and Japan. A goal without a measure (for example, "Become the best") is only a slogan. After goals are established, key strategies to support these goals are developed by the senior management team. The critical next step is open communication and dialogue that ultimately involves everyone in the organization.

The communication begins at the top level of management and cascades throughout the organization, level by level. The senior management team first discusses its goals and strategies with its direct reports (the second level of management) to ensure understanding and acceptance of the goals and strategies. This communication also includes discussion of the process capability, resource requirements, and implementation strategy of the second level of management, which will take responsibility for senior management's goals. This discussion between senior management and the second level of management must continue until both agree on the goals and the means to achieve them. Goals may be modified or resource allocations adjusted, as necessary. Once top-level managers and the second-level managers agree, the second-level managers begin the communication-negotiation process with their direct reports, which continues until these two levels reach agreement. This process continues throughout the remaining levels of the organization to ensure that everyone understands the goals, agrees to them, and has the resources and plans to carry them out.

An analogy used recently by an executive from Baldrige Award winner Texas Instruments Defense Systems applies here: Give all the employees penlights, show them how to turn the lights on, and empower them to do so. When they turn the penlights on, the beams of light will point in all directions. The power of illumination from all of these lights will be diffused across space. However, if those lights are aligned—focused on one defined target—there will be laser-like illumination on the target.

It is important not to confuse this desired alignment with a restriction on creativity. The employees are free to create new approaches or projects, as long as these projects contribute to the achievement of the business goals.

Putting the customer first

When a business finds itself in financial difficulty, often the employees suffer through expense cuts or layoffs. Customer needs are sacrificed for financial benefit. In effect, prolonged agony has been substituted for the crisis. A business that has demoralized employees and dissatisfied customers (each reinforces the other) is doomed.

A trade-off need not be made between customers, employees, and business results. TQM preaches that customer satisfaction is why a business exists. Motivated, empowered employees are the way to achieve customer satisfaction. If a business has satisfied employees and customers, business results will follow.

Courageous leadership is the key. It must create a supportive environment. Rewards and recognition, training, management role models, and communications must align to support the TQM initiatives. Everyone in a business has a responsibility for quality and an important role to play. Each must play his or her part and must not interfere with the roles of others.

First-line people, especially the employees who deal directly with customers, must operate according to agreed-upon processes and exercise continual improvement efforts. They should be empowered and encouraged to develop process changes under their control to continually simplify their work processes and focus their outputs on the needs of their customers.

Middle management must support the first line. It must also constantly seek to improve the processes for which it is responsible. Middle managers must actively seek to understand and eliminate root causes of customer dissatisfaction. They should allocate resources to teams that will provide the highest customer-oriented payoff.

Senior management must focus its attention on the initiation and support of major breakthroughs in selected areas. It should ensure the alignment of middle managers and first-line employees and support their efforts. Senior managers must be available to hear customer complaints about the system. This exposure to customer complaints increases management's sensitivity for identifying high-priority breakthrough initiatives.

Functional boundaries, barriers, and barbed wire

There are ways organizations can break down traditional functional boundaries, even when these barriers seem insurmountable.

Where known problems exist and repeated attempts at solutions have failed, it is a result of a breakdown in a cross-functional process. In the earlier years of implementing its quality system, Xerox discovered that using a natural work team would solve problems more effectively. These teams were effective when problems existed within an organization that had minimal outside influences. Unfortunately, sometimes this phenomenon is not the real world of an enterprise. The real value of teams occurs when they are truly cross-functional. That is where the most significant problems are solved, with the greatest financial payback.

Cross-functional team building leads to the empowering management behaviors necessary for process ownership. In order to be truly customer-focused, process owners need to be identified and held accountable for cross-functional processes that are most important for delivering products and services to customers. The dynamics of team effectiveness become more influential on the business when cross-functional teams interact, solving problems that cut across functions, organizations, and processes.

Process focus

During its quality journey, Xerox realized that it could improve its work processes to produce continuous improvement in results. Xerox found that although it was striving to become **The Document Company**, most of its work processes were not documented. It also did not use many in-process measures to assess the capability of its processes.

In response, Xerox decided to focus management attention on driving process improvements with the objective of improving business results. In order to help senior managers understand and internalize the power of this concept, they participated in the "red bead" experiment perfected by Dr. W. Edwards Deming. (Those who have participated in the "red bead" experiment realize that a statistically projectable number of red beads will always be drawn from the sample and that it is virtually impossible to draw all white beads without changing the make-up of the sample.) During this exercise, senior managers teased their CEO for not getting enough white beads out of the box. This exercise, although humorous, was a powerful learning experience about variability in processes. It persuaded senior management to buy into the more disciplined components of process improvement: documentation, standardization, process control, improvement goals, cycle time reduction, and variability reduction. These concepts were used to create a training program for work process improvement called Management By Fact.

Teams: directed diversity

Businesses are becoming companies of teams, progressing toward an end point characterized by teams of companies. In the past decade, Xerox has experienced the challenges associated with the formation and operation of teams made up of diverse groups of people. It has also seen the tremendous results that such teams deliver.

Generally, teams can overcome the barriers that have been constructed between functions, divisions, and management levels. Teams can bridge the gaps between companies and customers, companies and suppliers, and companies and companies.

Diversity of opinion, background, and skill brings power to teams. At Xerox, every October, there is a celebration called Teamwork Day. Simultaneously, in Rochester, New York; Dallas, Texas; and El Segundo, California, hundreds of Xerox quality teams discuss their projects with thousands of invited guests and Xerox people. All of this is organized and implemented by Xerox employees without management direction. Attendance at one of these events dispels any doubt that teams of diverse people can work together in harmony and can produce powerful outputs of value to customers, employees, and stakeholders.

The initial QIT that developed the Xerox Leadership Through Quality strategy was a diverse team from different functions and geographic areas. Their work output included elements that fostered the subsequent development of excellent team skills and performance.

Two key elements devised by the Quality Implementation Team produced surprising and rewarding results worldwide. The first is common tools. The fact that 100,000 people, worldwide, use the same six-step Problem Solving Process (see Figure 7.1) and meeting management approach is a very powerful enabler. Today, teams of people from any function, anywhere in the world, can join together with a common goal and immediately set to work solving a problem, without discussing the process they will use. At Xerox, we have found that a systematic approach to problem solving is a vital enabler toward becoming a successful quality practitioner. Teams will appoint a facilitator, a scribe, a time keeper, and even a behavioral checker. The responsibility of each role and its value are accepted and understood. The Xerox worldwide communications network enables team members located in different parts of the world to work together and communicate electronically, resulting in greater efficiency and cost savings.

The Xerox experience with teams has grown to include customers and suppliers, who form true partnerships with Xerox people to produce mutually beneficial outputs. Often, customers and suppliers are trained in

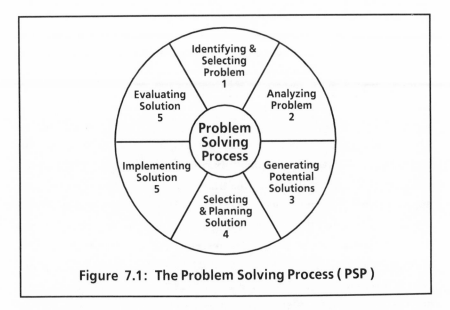

Figure 7.1: The Problem Solving Process (PSP)

the use of Xerox processes and tools so that they speak the same "language" as their Xerox teammates.

Xerox and the Amalgamated Clothing and Textile Workers Union also have been full partners in the quality journey since the beginning. Teams of union people and teams of union and nonunion people have contributed greatly to the company.

The common quality language and tools are powerful enablers for teams. Any concerns about the stifling of individual creativity by the standardized processes are ill-founded. People are free to fix anything that is broken or build anything that is needed. They have been given a quality "tool box"; however, they are not allowed to spend their precious time and energy inventing new tools.

Teach and you shall learn

Like many organizations, Xerox practiced the traditional approach to training: assemble the students in the classroom, teach the course, and return the students to their usual environment. This traditional approach, when applied to quality skills and behavior training, has a short half-life.

The unique training strategy of Learn-Use-Teach-Inspect substantially reduced the time-to-market of the Leadership Through Quality learning experience. There were several reasons for its success.

First, people in a natural work team were trained together as a unit. This approach ensured that all team members had the same training and enabled the team to talk about its mission, objectives, and customers—often for the first time.

Second, managers delivered part of the training, assisted by a training professional. To avoid potential embarrassment, managers had to thoroughly prepare before delivering the training to their respective teams. This approach served as a review of course material for managers and reinforced the notion that the manager, playing an active role as instructor, was evolving into the team's "coach." The inspection activity that occurred after training reinforced the coaching role of the manager. The manager would ask probing questions to determine if the teams were applying the training in an effective manner to their work processes.

However, the Learn-Use-Teach-Inspect training method could not be complete without providing for the training of newly hired employees. No Xerox employee is exempt from the experience of combining the learning with the practical application of TQM techniques. The sooner a new employee is trained, the more effective he or she will be in exhibiting role model behaviors.

Seek a broad spectrum of TQM applications

Much has been written about the application of TQM to manufacturing. Many companies have successfully used TQM in this area, and their experience can be valuable to companies that want to implement TQM techniques. But there are not many published examples in open literature about the deployment of TQM into the total organization: areas such as legal, marketing, sales, or accounting. Xerox developed its own extensions of TQM beyond manufacturing based on internal discoveries and "creative imitation" of benchmarking partners who shared their own process improvement developments. TQM has been slow to surface in these business support areas, not because people in these disciplines are obstinate or slow to learn, but because the processes and procedures they use tend to be batch-oriented rather than continuous. Statistical tools such as control charts are not commonly found in their workplace, nor are they commonly taught in college courses related to these fields.

Over the years, a "subculture" may have developed in these areas. It is characterized by a reverence for individuality, with incentives and reward systems designed to recognize individual competitiveness and accomplishment. The citizens of these subcultures often have no technical background so their problem-solving approaches tend to be instinctive rather than analytic.

Like most of us, sales and marketing people think of themselves as unique, and expect to be treated as such. They tend to resist attempts to get them to use standard processes or rules of conduct. Yet, teamwork is a critical enabler to the success of modern business. To summarize:

- Results are what we all seek.

- Results are the outputs of processes.

- Most critical business processes operate across functional boundaries.

- Only cross-functional teams can address problems with such processes in order to optimize results.

- Common practices, problem-solving tools, and common language facilitate and accelerate the performance of teams.

It is important that standard processes and a common language of quality be applied in individualistic business areas, but some individuality should be respected and preserved. However, some customization of processes by individuals or groups should also be allowed. For instance, Xerox allowed its United States sales organization to make a unique adaption of the nine-step Quality Improvement Process (see Figure 7.2), which is a basic tool used by Xerox people worldwide, to its sales process.

The sales organization adapted the QIP to make it the basic process used by sales representatives. The process starts with the development of an output statement or account goal; the identification of decision-makers or customers; and the gathering of requirements from the customer. The sales representative then develops action plans to satisfy each of the identified requirements. This activity represents the first four steps of a nine-step

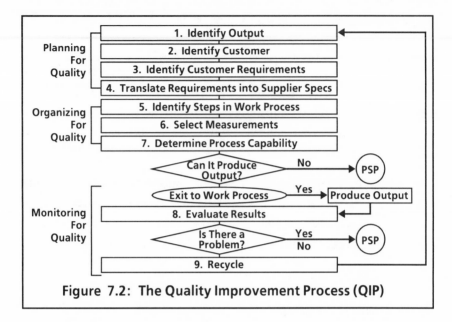

Figure 7.2: The Quality Improvement Process (QIP)

process. The sales force calls this process the Xerox Account Management Process (XAMP). It is essentially the same as the Xerox Quality Improvement Process, except for the substitution of some common sales terms for quality terms used in the QIP. If asked, "Do you use the QIP process in your daily work?", most sales representatives would say "No." But if asked, "Do you use XAMP?", virtually all would say "Yes."

The Xerox technical service organization accepted the concept of TQM more readily than the sales organization did. Service people tend to be

disciplined, and they use the scientific method every day as they diagnose and resolve equipment problems. They regularly use standard problem-solving tools, both the training material and the statistical process analysis tools. However, they resisted adopting the new quality processes developed by Xerox: "Why the change? I solve problems every day and have done so for years. Who needs a six-step process?" Yet, here too, in this nonmanufacturing area, TQM has been accepted and proven useful.

At Xerox, TQM philosophies, tools, and practices produce the same remarkable improvements in customer satisfaction, employee motivation, and business results worldwide. This is true for all functions, manufacturing and nonmanufacturing alike. A sensitivity to the individual needs of people is required—balanced by the conviction that common language and common tools are powerful quality enablers.

The use of a common quality language and tools can also alleviate functional differences. In 1986, a decision was made to appoint a new vice president of marketing. The person appointed did not have sales experience; he was chosen because he was a role model of TQM. Even though he was not from the sales culture, he had demonstrated an ability to understand and respect the contributions of sales and marketing people. His mission was to enhance the performance of sales and marketing through the use of TQM, without destroying the vibrant and aggressive spirit of the group. Under this direction, a quality marketing group emerged and produced powerful marketing outputs (such as the successful Xerox Total Satisfaction Guarantee), achieved record levels of employee motivation and satisfaction, and first and foremost, produced satisfied internal and external customers.

In summary, as TQM is rolled out, you will hear some standard objections:

- We're different.

- It won't work here.

- We don't have time.

People are diverse, and this diversity should be preserved. Be flexible in your adaptation of TQM. Recognize and appreciate the value of the diversity which exists. But these people still can use common tools and have common goals. With the adoption of TQM, the entire enterprise will continuously improve.

Everything we do communicates

The Quality Implementation Team that developed Leadership Through Quality was creating an internal revolution around quality. The concept of revolution is significant in that communication is essential to a successful revolution. Throughout the implementation of the quality strategy, Xerox focused on reinforcing key beliefs and sharing positive news about Leadership Through Quality to stimulate support for it. The Xerox director of communications ensured that senior management speeches, videos, and presentations included the quality theme to provide continuous reinforcement.

Behavior of the Xerox senior management team was the most important communication vehicle. Actions and behaviors communicate more powerfully than words. This concept is exemplified by Robert Galvin, CEO of Motorola. During a meeting of Motorola senior management, Galvin was frustrated because customer satisfaction was the last item on the quarterly review agenda. Therefore, he put customer satisfaction at the top of the agenda; following this review, he got up and left before the discussion on financial results. This sent a powerful message within Motorola regarding the emphasis on customer satisfaction. Starting every operations review with a discussion of customer satisfaction shows the importance of this topic in the spectrum of business priorities.

Key messages, such as the importance of customer satisfaction, must be repeated again and again. One frustration often expressed by senior managers is the need to repeat messages already delivered. It is essential for managers to understand that messages delivered one time do not stick. The constant drumbeat on an issue is necessary to instill the message in employees.

Traditionally, Xerox has launched major changes in direction with high-intensity advertisement campaigns. The company took a different approach with the Leadership Through Quality initiative to avoid the appearance that Leadership Through Quality was the latest management "whim." The new quality strategy was not announced with great fanfare; instead, the company focused on effective, organized implementation. Xerox was also cautious in external communications. It was not until about 1987 that Xerox began to talk publicly about the quality journey within the company. Its public advertising efforts did not refer to the quality movement until after the Business Products and Systems organization won the Baldrige Award.

Xerox did not create a stand-alone communication vehicle on the topic of quality, because it did not want employees to believe that quality was something over and above their normal job. Quality is an essential part of their daily job.

The value of quality networks

Although line management is fully accountable for the success of TQM, a separate, yet integrated, quality network provides invaluable support in many ways, especially during the vital implementation stages. Most importantly, it provides a parallel communications link to the enterprise. In other words, a quality network is a failsafe mechanism to communicate strategies simultaneous to line management's communication efforts. The quality network's communication activities are not a replacement for management communications; they supplement this process.

With the original Quality Implementation Team, the network actually took on the role of becoming the catalyst for change. Individual members of the network served as management conscience and behavioral barometer to their managers; collectively, this operation of the network turned their observations into actionable strategies for the total enterprise.

A quality network does not need to be a large staff of quality professionals. With line management ultimately accountable for quality, quality managers play an important fiduciary-like responsibility for product, service, and process quality assurance. These networks were generally made up of a balance of people with technical expertise in TQM as well as high potential, upwardly mobile line managers.

Some Xerox line senior managers were hesitant to place their best people in these jobs, driven by the perception that it would hurt mainline operations. It is necessary, however, to consistently select the best people for quality support positions, and for the sake of the personal growth of these people, rotate them to another assignment after two to three years. Supported by a small cadre of quality professionals, quality managers chosen from line management, who are placed strategically throughout the organization, can form a powerful alliance with line managers for TQM implementation.

Quick fixes don't work

"Ready, fire, aim" will not get results.

Patience is a virtue; aggressive patience makes the difference. Japanese companies tend to use a ten-year approach for their planning process and will make short-term sacrifices for the long-term gain—this is counter to the

Western culture and the short-term measurement sticks used in business: quarterly financial results and annual performance figures.

In developing its quality-improvement strategy and defining what needed to be accomplished, Xerox underestimated the difficulty of achieving its goals. It is easier and faster to define a desired state than it is to achieve it. However, the eighteen months spent designing the Xerox strategy for change and defining the approach was key for ensuring that the strategy could be implemented.

The objectives and strategy for Leadership Through Quality did not need to change during implementation, because it was a very insightful, comprehensive plan. However, the timing of the implementation plan, as originally envisioned, was adjusted to reflect the reality of the significant change that was required.

It is critical to deal with holdouts and nonconformists from the start. Failure to deal with them sends the wrong signal. However, time must be allowed for change to occur, and people change at different rates. Organizations also change at different rates, as do segments within organizations. In one of the early assessments of Leadership Through Quality progress, there was a high correlation between an organization's outstanding progress and its senior leadership taking ownership and using the tools and principles of quality.

Once quality processes are implemented, progress can come rapidly. For example, it took almost three years for Leadership Through Quality training to get started within the United States Marketing Group (USMG), a 32,000-person organization. While some field organizations heard of Leadership Through Quality in 1984 and began their study, the formal training for USMG senior managers did not occur until 1986. However, only three years later, this same organization played a key role in the successful pursuit of the Baldrige Award. This demonstrated an acquired maturity in the quality process over a very short time.

Conclusion

Xerox benefited from many experiences and insights during its decade-long quality journey. A series of key events, such as the pursuit of the Deming Prize, the Baldrige Award, and the European Quality Award, heightened and accelerated the learning experience. Sharing some of the "lessons learned" may encourage and help others who have begun or will embark on the TQM journey. These lessons are summarized below, without any attempt at prioritization.

Interventions are essential

An unexpected lesson from the quality journey was the powerful influence of external interventions on the quality agenda. This insight occurred as a result of the Xerox experience with the Deming Prize in 1980. It realized that the Deming Prize process was a means to achieve TQM implementation. Without this external influence, Xerox would not have been so successful in its Fuji Xerox operations. This experience was repeated by Xerox units that applied for quality awards in the United Kingdom, France, and the Netherlands.

The Baldrige Award application process provided new energy to the Xerox total quality priority. The NQA process forced Xerox to review the principles, processes, and results achieved in quality from a customer perspective. Xerox senior managers were forced to prepare themselves to present statistical data to the NQA site visit team.

Xerox began to realize that the total quality journey was like pushing a wheelbarrow full of rocks up a hill. If the company stopped pushing, it would stop making progress and, eventually, it would retreat downhill as gravity took hold. External interventions can help with the job of pushing quality.

The most recent experience at Xerox with external intervention was the Rank Xerox Business Certification process in preparation for the European Foundation for Quality Management Award. While implementing this process, Xerox benefited from the cross-organizational inspection process that it used in Europe. For instance, Xerox line managers from Italy and Germany examined and certified the quality process in Spain.

Expectations must be raised

The role of management in selecting and establishing expectations for continuous improvement is vital to the success of quality improvement. For example, Xerox senior managers debated whether to establish a customer satisfaction target of 100 percent. Some managers believed that it was impossible to control all of the factors that influenced the opinion of the customer. Therefore, they argued, the idea of achieving 100 percent was impossible. Others said that achieving 100 percent customer satisfaction was statistically impossible. In the end, Paul Allaire maintained that Xerox would adopt a 100 percent target on the basis of a very simple concept: If Xerox selected a target of less than 100 percent, such as ninety-nine percent, it would be admitting that it had decided not to do all that it could to satisfy one percent of its customers. No manager at Xerox wanted to step up to the challenge of identifying the customers, by name, the company had decided not to satisfy. In accepting 100 percent customer satisfaction as the goal, all Xerox people were encouraged to develop a resentment for each and every event that causes a dissatisfied customer, rather than accepting a situation which is "only a one percent problem."

In addition to selecting the specific targets for continuous improvement, the company must create an environment where everyone is encouraged to identify and aspire to achieve the best possible results for the customer. Xerox found the benchmarking process to be a valuable tool in setting expectations. For example, benchmarking teams in the early 1980s worked to understand and close the huge gap in the product delivery process and unit manufacturing cost. At that time, Xerox found that it was off the benchmarks by a factor of 50-100 percent. Xerox people used the benchmarking process to identify what had to be done and to accept the high level of expectations that went along with the task.

A step beyond benchmarking is the concept of pushing the theoretical limit of what a process can produce in terms of quality, cost, and delivery time. In the early 1990s, Xerox began to look at process improvement using the concept of cycle time reduction to achieve time, cost, and productivity improvements. Xerox found the theoretical limit to be a valuable concept to operationalize the role that high expectations play in moving teams forward on behalf of the customer.

Progress is the destination

Xerox has not arrived at its ultimate desired "end state" of quality performance. Its experience with Leadership Through Quality has shown that the company must set challenging corporate priorities, define goals that close gaps in performance for key business measures, and empower teams to continually improve work processes to increase quality and productivity for Xerox customers. This is truly a race without a finish line, and Xerox looks forward to developing more "lessons learned" as its people press forward to achieve ever improving performance in work processes for the benefit of its customers and stockholders.

In the concluding chapter, Paul Allaire discusses the macro-level lessons learned and sets the direction of Xerox toward the year 2000.

Chapter Eight
Setting the Direction

Paul A. Allaire

Every so often it is important and instructive to step back from the daily activities of the business and reflect on where we have been, what we have learned, and where we are going. In February 1993, we celebrated the tenth anniversary of our Leesburg meeting, where twenty-five senior Xerox managers developed the principles of Leadership Through Quality that were later documented in the Green Book. To celebrate, we gathered the original Leadership Through Quality design team for a reunion and a time of reflection. During this event, we reexamined the operational definition of "the year of maturity" which we envisioned in 1983 and assessed our progress in both the quality activities of the company and the results achieved. The following list of activities and results reflects the accomplishments of our original vision since the 1983 launch of Leadership Through Quality:

Quality Activities
- Implementation of Leadership Through Quality in Xerox is complete.
- Xerox people worldwide are applying Leadership Through Quality processes as part of their normal work.
- Goals and actions for continuing quality improvement are fully integrated in the planning, management, and review processes.
- Teamwork, discipline, and patience continue to develop as characteristics of the Xerox culture and work style.
- All appraisal, recognition, reward, and promotion systems are used routinely to encourage and reinforce the focus on our customer and continued quality improvement.

Results
- The pursuit of quality improvement and customer satisfaction has become a way of life in Xerox.

- A behavioral shift—from aggression, attacking, and internal competition to supporting, sharing, and teamwork—has been achieved.
- Confidence in the corporation is widespread and consistent throughout all Xerox units.
- Xerox people are sharing in the benefits of Leadership Through Quality.
- Xerox management practices have become a world-class standard.
- Xerox and Leadership Through Quality have become synonymous in the eyes of our employees, customers, suppliers, shareholders, and the general public.
- Xerox products and services are rated superior by our customers and industry analysts.
- The results of the Leadership Through Quality actions have made significant contributions toward the achievement of long-term corporate objectives.
- The tools and language of quality have become a cultural glue that binds Xerox people everywhere.

Xerox has moved a long way toward this state of maturity since the implementation of Leadership Through Quality. It took almost five years to get 100,000 Xerox employees trained in the processes of Leadership Through Quality, from the top corporate officers through the people on the front line. We went through a period of great change. We changed our measures. We introduced new tools, such as the Quality Improvement Process, and expanded upon others, such as employee involvement and benchmarking. We modified our appraisal and reward systems and aligned them to support the corporate priorities. We involved our people. And, we kept at it month after month and year after year. Now, even when the year of maturity seems to be just around the corner, there is much more to be done.

Today, Leadership Through Quality has become a fundamental business practice. We have taken the lessons learned from Leadership Through Quality and continue to apply them in order to maintain our global leadership position. Yet, we find the effort required for business process improvement is never-ending, and total quality, as we initially defined it, is no longer sufficient to differentiate Xerox from its competitors.

Let us examine the company from two perspectives. Let us look back at the business results we have achieved through our emphasis on TQM, and look ahead toward our engagement of Xerox people in the continuous pursuit of business productivity improvements for the future.

A look back: Doing business with total quality

As I look back on the past ten years, I recognize that we have effected a major turnaround of a formerly sagging American business. Does a concentration on quality improvement lead to business improvement? I believe that the numbers speak for themselves. And nowhere is this more apparent than in the Xerox improvement trends for our four corporate priorities: customer satisfaction, employee satisfaction, market share, and return on assets.

Customer satisfaction

The accomplishment that brings us the greatest pride in this journey is our consistent performance in steadily improving customer satisfaction. In the 1970s and early 1980s, we were arrogant and did not have a keen interest in how satisfied our customers were with our products and services. One of the first steps in our quality journey was to begin measuring customer satisfaction in 1981. By 1985, we knew that we understood our problem and the nature of its root causes: we needed to focus our efforts more coherently on the customer. By 1987, our internal assessment of progress in implementing Leadership Through Quality indicated that even more emphasis had to be placed on the customer. In other words, we had to become obsessed with pleasing, even delighting, the customer. At that time, we had three equal priorities: return on assets, market share, and customer satisfaction. So we made customer satisfaction the number one corporate priority.

We reemphasized the focus on the customer in 1990, in conjunction with our post-Baldrige Quality Intensification. And we offered our customers an industry first—a Total Satisfaction Guarantee. Under this unique guarantee, customers can obtain a like-for-like exchange for any product with which they are not completely satisfied within three years of their purchase. All they need to do is ask. No hassle.

Today, the number of dissatisfied customers is less than two percent, and less than one-half percent have exercised the Total Satisfaction Guarantee. In addition, benchmarking surveys indicate that Xerox is in a leadership position in the area of customer satisfaction. Even so, we are not completely satisfied with this performance. There is no reason why any Xerox customer should be displeased. We continue to aggressively pursue our goal of obtaining 100 percent customer satisfaction.

Employee satisfaction and motivation

To satisfy our customers, we must also address the needs of our employees. Employee satisfaction is a leading indicator of customer satisfaction, since only positively motivated employees will provide the positive environment necessary to meet and exceed the expectations of our customers. We have proven this in both statistical studies and, perhaps more importantly, in practical experience.

Xerox employees have been our company's strength, especially over the past fifteen turbulent years. Our partnership with the Amalgamated Clothing and Textile Workers Union is recognized as a role model for cooperative labor-management relations. Xerox people take pride in their membership in the Xerox family, and our internal employee satisfaction numbers show that we are the benchmark for employee satisfaction in our industry.

Market share

In the late 1960s and early 1970s, Xerox owned the reprographics business with more than eighty-five percent market share. We had a unique product with the 914, the first plain paper copier, and had exploited it with a customer-oriented pricing policy, which allowed Xerox to become dominant in the market. We protected our market position with patents on our technology, and it looked like we were invulnerable. That was not the case. Legal actions by the Federal Trade Commission stripped us of our patent protection, and attacks by our competitors began to erode our market share. However, our focus on the customer—and our ability to back it up as we became practitioners of the Leadership Through Quality principles and methods over the next decade—allowed us to reverse this market share trend. Today, we like to say that we are one of only a few major United States companies targeted by the Japanese that has been able to win back market share, and we did it without any government support or protection. (By 1987, we had reversed the decline in our market share and began to recover market position.)

Today, it is a war. We are challenged by our principal competitors in almost every market. Only by aggressively satisfying every customer, one at a time, can we continue to regain our market position and outdistance the competition.

Return on assets

By the early 1980s, Xerox was in deep trouble. Foreign competition had cut our market share by half, our customers were not happy with us, and our return on assets had declined from the twenty percent range in the 1970s to below eight percent in a matter of a few years. In addition, our Japanese competitors were profitably selling products for what it cost us to manufacture them.

Regarding profitability, our return on assets has steadily improved since 1985, from a low of eight percent in 1983 to eleven percent in 1987, twelve percent in 1989, and almost fifteen percent in 1992. Such steady progress comes not only from providing customers with great products and services, but also from the elimination of waste and the ongoing efforts of our people in applying Leadership Through Quality.

Quality awards

In addition to our performance improvements in the four corporate business priorities, we have also received worldwide recognition for our efforts in the deployment of Leadership Through Quality by winning quality awards in many countries including: Australia, Belgium, Brazil, Canada, Columbia, England, France, Hong Kong, Ireland, Japan, Mexico, the Netherlands, the United States, and the European Quality Award.

Focusing on quality allowed us to survive in the 1980s and we used it to turn the company around. We involved our entire work force in becoming part of the solution. This means everyone—the senior team, middle management, and individual contributors. So today, all levels of management and all geographic areas are armed with quality tools and are able to face the challenges of the 1990s with confidence. This is the foundation upon which Xerox will build its future.

A look forward: Defining the "New Productivity"

As business continues to change and progress at a more rapid rate of development, keeping up with the demands of change becomes increasingly more challenging. The perceptions of productivity, so often relied upon in the past, simply do not suffice any longer.

In our post-industrial world, we cannot grow business productivity without growing the productivity of the white collar worker—the purpose of which is the building, sharing, and compounding of knowledge. As Roger Milliken said, "Insanity is doing things the same way and expecting a different outcome." And we know that in the fiercely competitive markets in which we operate, a fast, knowledgeable response to the customer's needs by the people closest to the action is critical, and will become even more critical in the future.

We must keep in mind, however, that in a free-market economy, competition is not only necessary, it is desirable. It spurs creativity, innovation, and progress, which feed both the consumer and producer sides of the economy.

Getting productivity from white-collar work means redefining productivity. Old productivity was defined in terms of volume and ignored value. It lost sight of the customer. New productivity is value-driven. It is anchored in the creation of knowledge, the elimination of waste, and the abandonment of unproductive work.

Xerox is focusing on the New Productivity for two reasons. First, we have to be productive for competitive reasons. We are competing with some of the most productive companies anywhere, and to succeed we will have to get world-class returns on all of our assets from our capital, our people, our position, and from our technology. Second, we have redefined the vision and strategic intent of Xerox. We now refer to ourselves as The Document Company. Whenever you have people involved in processes, you have documents. Because documents are integral to business, we must use document technology to enable productivity increases. Our customers have come to understand that. Xerox understands that. Together, we are exploring new frontiers of office productivity.

Our strategic intent is to be the leader in the global document market as the premier provider of document services which enhance business productivity. Xerox will be the leader of this industry by providing our customers with innovative, intelligent document services—products, systems, solutions, and support—to meet their current and anticipated requirements. Xerox services will enable individuals and organizations to be more effective and productive. We will base our leadership on superior document technologies that are linked to a superior understanding of the document and its role in our customer's business processes. And we will be supported worldwide by Xerox people who are dedicated to providing quality customer service.

Our founder, Joe Wilson, once commented: "In the long run, our customers are going to determine whether we have a job or not." This is still true today. Thus, our strategic intent could be simply paraphrased: Serve the document needs of our customers.

Our strategy is tied to helping our customers become more productive—using the document to enhance business processes. If we are to retain credibility, then we need to be an internal proof case and a showcase of document productivity. If we cannot demonstrate how we can become more productive, why should our customers believe our claims that we can help them? We can help our customers implement productive work communities by providing the technology for better information, knowledge, and collaboration, just as we are doing inside Xerox.

In order to create value for our customers, our future depends not only on our technological leadership, manufacturing muscle, and the high quality of our goods and services, but also on our ability to motivate and lead our people to create a new kind of productivity. Our strategic direction is linked to helping our customers and their customers become more productive. We are experimenting and learning, but we see some emerging patterns. Consistent and big gains in productivity—twenty-five percent to fifty percent—are achievable. We believe that there is the potential for a unique solution that can provide us with a competitive advantage in the global marketplace, which is not easily replicated. We see the new productivity as a "person-centric" approach, based on the belief that our most unique asset is our people and their ability to create value.

Total Quality enables the "New Productivity"

For Xerox, succeeding in an increasingly dynamic environment means doing so in the presence of global competitors and with a core technology that is migrating from light lens to digital at a very rapid rate. Therefore, we must combine the implicit values of TQM—discipline, uniformity, teamwork, and empowerment—with the intrinsic values of creativity—entrepreneurism, innovation, and diversity—in order to develop a renewed productivity and competitive advantage. To do this, we are focusing on making Xerox the most productive company in our industry, and ultimately one of the most productive companies in the world. Our intent is to pass this knowledge on to our customers by providing productive offerings and by sharing our insights and experience on TQM.

Without total quality, we would not be able to aspire to world-class productivity. Xerox must use all the expertise and experience we have gained from Leadership Through Quality by continuing to focus even more sharply on and driving breakthroughs in work process improvement and employee empowerment. We need improvement in both of these areas to make the organization more productive. Both efforts are necessary and neither is sufficient alone.

Our future direction includes reaffirmation of our dedication to Leadership Through Quality and our intention to continue to use the quality process to accomplish all our objectives. As The Document Company, we will continue to shape and lead the document services industry. This is the direction we intend to take for the foreseeable future. We need, on a worldwide basis, to generate profitable revenue growth and to become a showcase for productivity.

Xerox 2000: Making theory practical

I believe that by rethinking some basic concepts of how to organize work and resources, we can gain a competitive advantage by building on the special characteristics and strengths of our people. The approach we are using is called "productive work communities." This involves designing organizations to ensure a fit between work, people, information, and technology. We call them productive work communities because our objective is to create natural work groups, centered around natural units of work, which can develop into communities of practice, work, and learning.

The eight strategies implemented by this approach include the following:

- Micro-enterprise units: Redesign work units so that they encompass whole work processes as much as possible within the core work team.

- Self-management: Empower people to design/redesign their own work processes and practices, including work flows and assignments. Take supervisory roles out where possible (one manager might have a number of teams day-by-day), and train the manager to be a coach, consultant, supporter, and resource person.

- Multifunctional people: Encourage and reward people to learn different skills. This not only makes people a more valuable resource, but also provides teams with the ability to reconfigure themselves. It also builds learning into the job, which is in itself a source of motivation and reward for individuals.

- Minimal but clear boundary conditions: Limit the number of outside constraints on the autonomy of the unit by focusing on a very small number of key processes inside the unit, as well as the unit's results.

- Organization design from the micro-enterprise unit out: Turn the process of organization design upside down. Instead of always designing top-down, start with the micro-enterprise unit that deals directly with the customer, product, and service, and then work outward.

- Gainsharing: Create systems that enable people to share the benefits of their efforts and creativity—not just financially, but also through recognition and growth.

- Continued application of quality tools: Have productive work communities employ quality tools to enhance their work and create process ownership. These tools become much more valuable when they can be applied to a whole work process, rather than just a small piece of it. This approach also cuts down on the number of Quality Improvement Teams needed to cope with cross-functional issues in order to mend the functional system.

- Use of information technology and knowledge-based work systems: Make intensive use of our document technology to support these new work communities—including knowledge-based work systems, documents with intelligence, networks, et cetera.

It is important to note that our ten years of quality application and the experience gained from thousands of cross-functional teams have armed us with the basic knowledge and skills to proceed with a boldness toward a "functionless" business environment. One key factor we have learned is that new productivity is enabled by empowering people to do what they inherently know is the right thing to do. Management must simply lead, set clear direction, provide the right coaching, information, and tools—and get out of the way. This is how we liberate the people who can create value for the customer. We see it as a universal challenge and a common pursuit for all business.

I recognize that it is easy to put together a list of desired dimensions and to exhort people to change. In reality, a change of this order is very, very difficult and time-consuming. We tend to focus on the hardware of organizational change because, ironically, it is easy to work on. Behavioral "software" is more difficult to change. The soft stuff really is the hard stuff.

World-class productivity goes hand-in-hand with this approach to working together, however. In fact, I believe that if we do not achieve our organizational goals, we will not attain the productivity we need. That is why we need to use quality to focus on creating a working environment within and between operational units that reflects these dimensions. And to do this, we must continue to move ahead on each of the following:

- First, break up the bureaucracy. Take out layers of management. Knock down the functional barriers. Streamline processes. Improve clockspeed. Push decision-making, responsibility, and accountability down to the people closest to the problems or to the customer. Empower our people.

- Second, invest in people. We have invested over twenty-five hundred man years in quality training during the 1980's and we are convinced that it is one of the better investments that we've ever made. We are continuing to make significant investments in worker training at all levels of the company.

- Third, build "communities of practice." These small, entrepreneurial units have the capacity to manage themselves. They raise the concept of Total

Quality Management to new heights. Each individual and each team has the freedom to act, the security to be bold, the motivation to succeed, and the opportunity to contribute.

- Fourth, build a learning organization—an environment in which learning is pervasive and second nature. Create an environment in which failures are seen as opportunities to learn, successes are studied with an eye on improvement, new ideas are cherished, nurtured, and implemented, and learning is defined as doing things differently and better.

- Fifth, enhance the use of information technology. Get people the right information at the right time. Combine information with experience and world class processes in order to act quickly and decisively.

To summarize, Xerox must use quality to create an environment where we are market-connected and action-oriented as we work to ensure we achieve absolute results—those that are measured in external business terms rather than against the plan. Moreover, we need to change how we work together for the good of the common team. We need to empower our people. We need to have open and honest communication, even if it causes embarrassment or discomfort and may not be the "news" that we wanted to hear. We need constructive conflict or productive collision, rather than collusion. We also need to create an environment where we are constantly reflecting on and learning from our experiences.

Xerox has traveled a long way on the total quality path in the past ten years. We are proud of our accomplishments, but we realize that there is much left to be done. As we look forward to the future, we believe it will be exciting, challenging, and dynamic. With our TQM foundation firmly under us, we are now building toward a new productivity, both that will benefit ourselves and our customers. We look forward to the year 2000 with a strong sense of mission, commitment, and confidence.

Index

Xerox Quality Services is a world-wide organization of quality practitioners. We deliver results-oriented quality consulting, training, facilitation and software to organizations committed to change and superior performance. We help our customers do what they do better, create value for their customers, achieve world-class business results, and become more competitive in the marketplace.

Many providers of quality support have discovered *What* must be done to implement a quality strategy. Xerox, however, is the only winner of the world's three most prestigious quality awards (the U.S. Malcolm Baldridge Award, the Deming Prize in Japan and the European Quality Award) as well as over 15 other national quality awards around the world. **Xerox Quality Services** offers its clients direct experience in *How* to successfully implement a strategy that produces measurable improvements in results.

Xerox Quality Services provides its clients with:
- *Consulting* on business transformation through strategic quality planning, business assessment and policy deployment.

- *Training* in basic and advanced quality topics including process improvement, problems solving, meeting effectiveness, teamwork, change management, leadership and human resource management. Trainer certification is also available.

- *Facilitation* of quality processes, providing hands-on expertise in specific areas including statistical tools, benchmarking, customer satisfaction, human resources and supplier management.

For more information contact:

In the United States:	**In Europe:**
Xerox Corporation	Xerox Quality Services
Unites States Customer Operations	Rank Xerox Limited (IHQ)
Xerox Quality Services	Parkway
100 Clinton Avenue South - 18B	Marlow
Rochester, NY 14644	Bucks SL7 1YL
USA	ENGLAND
1-800-438-5077	44-1628-893097

In Canada:
Xerox Quality Services
Xerox Canada Limited
33 Bloor Street East, 6th Floor
Toronto, Ontario M4W-3H1
CANADA
416-972-7056